A Non-Violent Resistance Approach with Children in Distress

A Non-Violent Resistance Approach with A Guide for Parents and Professionals Children in Distress

Carmelite Avraham-Krehwinkel and David Aldridge

Jessica Kingsley Publishers
London and Philadelphia

First published in 2010
by Jessica Kingsley Publishers
116 Pentonville Road
London N1 9JB, UK
and
400 Market Street, Suite 400
Philadelphia, PA 19106, USA

www.jkp.com

Library of Congress Cataloging in Publication Data
A CIP catalog record for this book is available from the Library of Congress

British Library Cataloguing in Publication Data
A CIP catalogue record for this book is available from the British Library

ISBN 978 1 84310 484 1

Printed and bound in Great Britain by
Athenaeum Press, Gateshead, Tyne and Wear

Contents

Introduction   7

Chapter One: The Politics of Family Conflict   9

Chapter Two: An Ecological Approach   13

Chapter Three: The Non-Violent Resistance Model   33

Chapter Four: From Theory to Practice: The Intervention   43

Chapter Five: A Young Child with Self-Destructive
Behaviour   48

Chapter Six: A Barricaded Teenager   62

Chapter Seven: A Teen at Risk   80

Chapter Eight: Family and Community   109

Chapter Nine: The Child, the Parent and the School   128

Chapter Ten: The Model of Non-Violent Resistance:
A Guidebook for Parents   142

Chapter Eleven: Overview   174

References   185

Index   189

Introduction

Throughout the Western world we are hearing different variations of the same problem. Children are increasingly violent with their parents and teachers. Families are disrupted and increasing numbers of children and teenagers are being denied access to school or are themselves refusing to be educated. Children and their parents are distressed and this spreads out to friends and family.

As we will see later, Mr and Ms Schmidt have three children. The youngest child, Thomas, has outbursts of violence at home and in the nursery and shows a total refusal to be disciplined, especially when the father is involved. Each exchange or argument culminates in alarming self-destructive and suicidal exclamations from Thomas. The parents are distraught. The situation escalates.

The same process happens with teenagers too. Mr and Ms Hernandez have a son called Robert who is 14 and a half, and two daughters, Diana, who is 11 and Yvonne, who is eight. The father emigrated from Spain and the mother is Swedish. Both parents work hard and often come back fairly late from work. In their absence a day care-taker looks after the children. Robert had begun to barricade himself in his room, turning day into night, refusing to attend school, do any home work or take any responsibility for household chores, drinking, and getting in with the 'wrong crowd'. He is verbally aggressive and physically abusive towards his sister and his mother.

As you will read, it is often the vulnerable and helpless mother who appeals for help with a child who has become impossible. All of the blame is put upon the shoulders of the teenager, who is seen as aggressive, manipulative and risk-taking. However, when the mother employs the Non-Violent Resistance approach, she begins to see her child differently. When the mother abandons her helplessness, the child is unburdened as well.

For example, Mrs Halpern is in her mid-forties and is a secretary by profession but presents herself as a housewife and as a single mother of ten children. She is widowed and has reached breaking point. She complains of deep distress and extreme difficulties with the nine children presently living at home. Two of her children – 16-year-old Daniel and seven-year-old Asher – are showing signs of violence and have severe emotional outbursts. Mrs Halpern finds herself confronted by her husband's extended family who reject her, claiming that she brought about the death of their son. The son, Daniel, holds on tightly to his father's memory, to the extent that he even wears his father's clothes. Together with his father's family, he bears marked hostility to his mother, claiming that she stole his father's life. Slowly, Mrs Halpern finds herself alienated from her late husband's family and from her community. The ten children are torn between their loyalty to their mother and their father and his family. During this period, the children display a wide range of symptoms: depression, not being able to wake up in the morning for work or school, intolerable physical and verbal outbursts, and tantrums among the younger children. The impact of the ongoing events leaves its strongest mark on Daniel, the 16-year-old.

There is a need then for an intervention that will negotiate peace among the family for the benefit of the child. This model of Non-Violent Resistance offers a basis for offering help to the individual as they live their lives within the family and within the community. This approach has been used by parents, professionals and teachers.

NOTE
The word 'child' is used to describe children of both genders. For reasons of convenience, both boys and girls are referred to using the pronouns 'he' or 'him'.

CHAPTER ONE

The Politics of Family Conflict

This work began eight years ago. The underlying motivation that led to this book was the urgent need for a realistic, practical and efficient parental approach that can be applied within the field of behavioural problems. What we are talking about in this book is family politics – politics with a small 'p' but nevertheless politics, politics being any attempt to influence, coerce or manipulate the behaviour of another person in a network of relationships.

A search through the vast professional literature shows how intricate and multi-faceted the phenomenon of children with behavioural problems can be. In the literature, we find complex and versatile theories that are often interjected with similarly complex assumptions and methods of interventions – all aiming to tackle the problem, while acknowledging how difficult, if not impossible, the task is. Despite all differences, one fact appears to be common to all theories – that children with behavioural problems are more difficult to access for treatment. Even the more serious interventions report not only on the difficulties of maintaining treatment, but also of bringing that treatment to conclusion. Reports show that the older the child, the higher the drop-out rate. Similarly, the success of treatment decreases as the age increases; that is, the older the child the less chance of treatment success (Dishion and Patterson 1992; Kazdin, Holland and Crowley 1997; Patterson, Dishion and Chamberlain 1993).

In our earlier work, revolving around the design of a new working model, we resolved to meet two basic conditions:

1. The working model we developed should aspire to high ethical standards in viewing the child's needs and resolving the problem.

2. The model could be implemented in spite of the child's resistance, his non co-operation or even his absence from the therapy, without compromising his physical, mental or social well-being.

This was the background for the formulation of the Non-Violent Resistance Model that we present in this book. The model is designed as a short-term intervention that targets parents of children with severe disruptive behaviours, generally diagnosed as conduct disorder and oppositional defiant disorder, and is based on the ethical stance and concepts found in the Non-Violent Resistance movement (Avraham-Krehwinkel 2003; Bruyn and Rayman 1979).

Non-Violent Resistance developed as a concept within the confines of world-wide social political struggle. Among its advocates were Gandhi and Martin Luther King. The central principles that characterize the Non-Violent Resistance approach are: (1) avoiding violent reactions (Sharp 1960, 1973); (2) realizing that continued struggle is necessary; (3) creating transparency of the struggle; (4) recruiting support and (5) taking unconditional reconciliatory action (Bruyn and Rayman 1979).

Basic ideas found in the Non-Violent Resistance Model were also derived from the coercion theory (Patterson *et al.* 1984; Patterson, Reid and Dishion 1992). It defines the central issue, innate to the relationship between the parent and child with disruptive behaviour, as the struggle over dominance and the ensuing confusion over the hierarchy of roles within the family (Bugental *et al.* 1993; Bugental and Happaney 2000; Bugental, Lyon, Krantz and Cortez 1997; Chamberlain and Patterson 1995). This struggle tends to be stubborn and persistent, resulting in mutual ever-expanding cycles of escalation, which become the common ground for the parent–child relationship (Borduin *et al.* 1995; Cairns, Santoyo and Holly 1994; Cavell 2001; Dishion, French and Patterson 1995; Moffitt 1993a, 1993b; Rothbart and Bates 1998). Avenues of communication narrow into a cascade of arguments, threats, screams, admonitions and at times physical attacks, all ultimately leading to deterioration and detachment.

The Non-Violent Resistance Model takes as its basis the escalation that exists in nearly every scenario involving children with destructive behaviour. This escalation of demands breeds hostility and parents surrender to their child's demands, aggravating and amplifying the child's insistence and aggression. Such escalation results either in parental apathy or in parental outbursts that they later regret. The outcome of these pendulum swings can be severe for child and parent alike (Patterson *et al.* 1992). Parent–child relations are perpetuated by processes of escalatory action and reaction. These maladaptive processes begin to erode the child's developmental progress, distorting parental image and authority (Minuchin 1974). This distortion feeds on helplessness, resulting in confusion, guilt and anxiety. These attributes of helplessness become both cause and effect, reflected in every action and reaction by both parent and child.

The model we use here draws upon an eco-systems approach (Aldridge 1999; Bronfenbrenner 1979, 1986, 1989), which maintains that parents and children operate within multiple environments – ranging from the nuclear to the extended family, and including circles of friends and acquaintances, the school and the broader community. Aldridge's model of an eco-systemic management of distress is one of the main foundations on which the Non-Violent Resistance Model operates and affords the advantage of redefining seemingly maladaptive delinquent acts by the child as acts of attempted problem resolution intended to promote change. We also emphasize the idea of reconciliation by drawing from the field of ethology (de Waal 1993) and by identifying gestures of reconciliation as central to the process of de-escalation and the resolution of conflicts (Keltner and Potegal 1997).

The Non-Violent Resistance Model surveys the family panoramically – its roles and the relations assigned to its members – as part of a social, cultural and political ecology. This perception assigns to the individuals involved, the parents, the children and the exchanges negotiated among them, an importance that goes beyond the confines of the times and places specific to any particular events that have occurred (Aldridge 1999).

The restoration of autonomy, authority and legitimacy to parental action is the target of the Non-Violent Resistance Model. Fulfilling this target will enable the healthy development of the child. The Non-Violent Resistance Model holds within it the promise of reaching this target as the values it espouses are shared by parents and professionals alike.

In this book we aim to unfold the theoretical nature of the problem, portray the beginning of the model's ideas and follow its development to a fully applicable and viable working model that qualifies as an evidence-based treatment. We present some of the cases as they developed in the course of the intervention according to the Non-Violent Resistance Model.

Between 2000 and 2003, we conducted a study in three phases, termed Study A, B and C (Avraham-Krehwinkel 2005), that was designed to test the applicability and efficacy of the Non-Violent Resistance Model within the framework of a short-term intervention. Included within the study target group were parents of children with severe disruptive behaviours generally diagnosed as conduct disorder and oppositional defiant disorder. The goal of the intervention was to enable and empower parents to cope with the child's disruptive behaviour. All three studies applied a short-term psychotherapeutic intervention consisting of four to five sessions, each lasting one hour.

The applicability and efficacy of the Non-Violent Resistance Model within the framework of a short-term intervention was apparent in all the three stages. The results demonstrate that the fully tested therapeutic procedure of the Non-Violent Resistance Model is indeed a viable technique for addressing the problem of escalation and reducing distress – the cardinal issues in relationships between parents and children with behavioural problems. The results also demonstrate that this approach is applicable in everyday clinical practice.

CHAPTER TWO

An Ecological
Approach

What we all search for as parents is an appropriate parental style that
will facilitate and support the natural and optimal growth of the child
within the family. If we look at the literature, we find a varied spectrum
of educational approaches that are, more often than not, contradictory
in nature. Every approach promotes one specific parental style that it
purports is 'right' for raising children – to ultimately provide control
and mastery over anti-social behaviour.

At one end of the spectrum lies the authoritarian approach. This
approach seeks to establish parental authority through the use of
power, discipline and rigid punitive means – physical and verbal – in
an attempt to control the child with problematic behaviour (Baumrind 1991; Chamberlain and Patterson 1995). At the other end of
the spectrum lies the modern permissive approach. This approach
attempts to minimize manipulative intervention in the child's natural
and healthy development. Some parents are ideologically opposed to
exerting authority over their children in general, and object specifically to punishment (Baumrind 1991; Eisenberg and Murphy 1995;
Olweus 1980.)

The results of many empirical studies provide ample support for
a common cultural-sociological perception maintaining that there is a
unidirectional causal link that sees parents as the source and cause of
the problematic behaviour displayed by the child (McCord, McCord
and Zola 1959). The child is perceived as the sole victim in the family.
Such parents are characterized as severe, rigid and violent and they
demonstrate little affection towards their child.

PARENTAL STYLES

There is a relationship between a severe, rigid, authoritarian parental style and the extreme, aggressive reaction of the child. Aside from the question of its moral legitimacy, the disadvantage of this educational-parental approach is that it does not appear to be particularly effective. Attempts to establish parental authority through coercive rigid means are not only fruitless, they also serve to further degenerate the child's condition.

The liberal-permissive approach, which peaked in the Western world in the 1960s and 1970s, established the popular assumption that perceives the child as innately good (Miller 1981, 1985). Setting limits and controlling the child's behaviour is perceived as a rough manipulation of the child's natural course of development. In addition, the child's right to privacy is cultivated as a supreme value. These views strengthen the belief that restricting or frustrating the child's desires is at the root of his destructive behaviour (Elkind 1994; Parsons 1965). Central to the permissive approach is the child and the maximal satisfaction of his needs. The parent is expected to provide a supportive environment where the child can express his needs and impulses, releasing him from any constraints or worries about the outcome of his actions (Farson 1974; Neill 1964; Spock and Parker 1998). When faced with children who enjoy unlimited freedom, however, parents demonstrate great difficulty in functioning effectively. Lack of parental control takes the child out of immediate supervision, leaving him ignorant and unaware of his impact on the 'worlds' he inhabits – whether they be friends, places or activities. The child has clearly defined 'worlds' which are off-limits for parents and other adults – a circle of friends, certain places that he frequents and activities that he engages in. At the same time lack of parenting, which may result from overwork, illness, stress or lack of interest in the child, exposes a parental weakness that will inevitably be utilized by the 'unmonitored child', and result in escalation at home and in the expression of extreme behaviours (Kazdin 1996; Patterson 1983). Escalation is used to describe an increase in anger, anxiety and help-lessness, resulting in ever heightening, harsh responses on the part of parent and child alike.

A third pattern is the pendulum pattern. Swinging back and forth between yielding to the child's wishes and exerting extreme control through punitive means creates a spiral of escalating extreme reactions on both sides – parent and child alike. The two extremes – giving in on the one hand, and severe punishment on the other hand – strengthen the child's belief that increasing his own aggression will produce the much desired parental submission (Bandura 1969, 1973; Chamberlain and Patterson 1995; Patterson 1976, 1982).

ANTI-SOCIAL BEHAVIOUR: NATURE OR NURTURE?

Anti-social behaviour appears in the literature as a phenomenon emerging in early childhood that is likely to be stable, persistent and continuous throughout a lifetime (Kazdin 1996; Martin, Wisenbaker and Huttuenen 1994; Pepler and Rubin 1991; Thomas and Chess 1977). There is a continuing nurture versus nature debate about the causes of challenging behaviour. This can be condensed to the questions 'Are we born deviant?' or 'Are we made deviant by those around us?' In some way this is a Shakespearean perspective, as Malvolio says in *Twelfth Night* 'Some are born great, some achieve greatness and others have greatness thrust upon them' (Act II, Scene 5, line 159). Maybe we could substitute the word 'deviance' for 'greatness'. In this chapter we will present a short overview of that debate.

Genetics and environmental factors combine to create anti-social behaviour (Moffitt 1993a, 1993b; Rende 1993; Rende and Plomin 1992). Many researchers claim to have identified an unmistakable link between a neuropsychological deficit and anti-social behaviour – beginning in early childhood and exhibiting continuity through mid-childhood into adolescence (Lynam, Moffitt and Stouthamer-Loeber 1993; Moffitt 1990; Tremblay *et al.* 1991). Two kinds of neurological deficit are associated empirically with anti-social behaviour: verbal and operative deficits. There is a general claim that cognitive deficits and anti-social behaviour share a variance that is independent of social status, race, motivation or academic achievement. We also know that the genetic problem of Fragile X is a contributory factor for attention disorders in children (Hagerman and Hagerman 2002).

Aggressive children

Aggressive children tend to minimize and ignore information that could be relevant when interpreting the intentions of another child, causing them to concentrate on the hostility of the other child and interpret his actions as hostile. This misinterpretation then becomes habitual, taking an automatic course. These children feel empowered by the strong responses that their behaviour generates and they tend to underestimate its negative consequences – both on them and on those with whom they are interacting. This combination of the aggressive child's experience, his environment and his temperament can determine persistent anti-social behaviour (see Table 2.1). This behaviour does not only result from how one controls the child, but also from the interactions he himself creates with his environment. Although aggressive exchanges appear in almost every family (Chamberlain and Patterson 1995), we can identify those families that experience them very frequently, which in turn provide the child with a foundation to practice anti-social behaviour and incorporate it into his development. The child learns to use aggression in order to extend his control over his environment, displaying and activating this pattern automatically in other settings and with other people.

TEMPERAMENT

From a neuropsychological perspective, temperament is defined as that aspect which accentuates individual characteristics and distinguishes anti-social children or adolescents from others. The characteristic phenomena of an individual's emotional nature is dependent upon constitutional make-up and, therefore, is largely hereditary in origin. If there is a lack of compatibility between the temperament characteristics of the child and that of his parents then problems may occur. Bates, Freeland and Lounsbury (1979) point out that a difficult temperament apparent at six months can be used as prognosis for boys' and girls' extreme behaviour in mid-childhood (Bates *et al.* 1991). Olweus' work (1987), as well as Magnusson's (1988), shows that children who exhibit problematic behaviour differ from other children by displaying a physiological need for higher levels of arousal as seen in their higher testosterone, adrenaline and cortisol levels – all of which are associated with stress. The neuropsychological discussion also assumes that hereditary characteristics are responsible for the anti-social phenomenon.

One of the most difficult problems associated with anti-social behaviour is its persistence. In spite of the fact that the neuropsychological approach explains many aspects of anti-social behaviour, the question of the origin of its persistent nature remains unanswered. Among professionals, anti-social behaviour is considered extremely difficult and challenging, even for those parents who are affectionate and resourceful (Quay 1987). As such, the assumption underlying the neuropsychological approach, that perceives anti-social behaviour as persistent and stable, raises difficult questions as to the possible prognosis of change and healing.

Social interaction

As the personality and behaviour of an individual is shaped through interaction with his environment, many researchers point to the fact that this interaction can play a decisive role in both initially exciting anti-social behaviour and sustaining it throughout a person's lifetime (Bell and Chapman 1986; Caspi, Elder and Bem 1987; Mccoby and Martin 1983; Patterson 1982; Sameroff and Chandler 1975). Relationships are not only woven in endless numbers of interactions taking place between the individual and his surroundings, but they also shape his personality and his development. It is through social interaction that a person develops his first emotional bond and acquires the social context that will accompany him throughout the course of his life.

THE ATTACHMENT MODEL

The attachment model states that natural, unmediated and unconditional intimacy stems from the parent and child's willingness to establish an emotional bond during infancy and early childhood. These primary parent–child relationship patterns provide the emotional context for the later development of the child and adolescent (Lewinsohn, Rohde and Farrington 2000).

Parent–child relationships that are almost exclusively based on increasingly negative interactions narrow down the child's sense of being loved (Patterson and Dishion 1988; Patterson et al. 1992). Ultimately, such relationships lead to insecure intimate relations (Cicchetti and Lynch 1993). This is expressed in the slightest of gestures and nuances in everyday life. In other words, care-giving that involves failure, neglect and misinterpreting the urgency of the situation, undermines the attachment relationship between parent and child.

What is common to aggressive and anti-social behaviour is that both serve as a means for the individual to alter his environment. The problem of the child's anti-social behaviour does not only result from how one controls that child, but also from the interactions he himself creates with his environment (see Table 2.1 for a list of typical characteristics of the anti-social child).

Aggressive exchanges appear in almost every family (Chamberlain and Patterson 1995). The child learns to use aggression in order to extend his control over his environment, displaying and activating this pattern automatically in other settings and with other people. In this coercive process, parents often demonstrate inconsistent efforts to put an end to these patterns. This is the prototypical behaviour that Chamberlain and Patterson (1995) define as parental inconsequence.

Aggressive exchanges damage the child's development and establish the progression of anti-social behaviour. The more the parent and child become caught up in this process, the less they can recognize the role they play in it and their detrimental contribution to it. They exhaust parental relationship skills, which include displays of affection and love towards the child. The child, in return, displays similar incompetence. Aggressive exchanges then rule out other alternatives of contact making.

Anti-social behaviour can originate through temper tantrums and physical abuse in the environment of young children. Preschool children confront their parents and succeed in getting what they are after. This, however, is only a short-term gain. As a result of this acquired strategy, the child is then unable to develop an alternative strategy that will allow him to delay his need for immediate satisfaction for the purpose of long-term goals. Patterson *et al.* (1992) also recognize that lack of obedience and ignoring authority are the main adaptive style of the anti-social child, acquired through numerous exchanges with his environment. With sufficient practice in aggressive behaviour the child will activate the same automatic techniques to achieve his demands in many new situations.

TABLE 2.1 TYPICAL CHARACTERISTICS OF THE CHILD WITH ANTI-SOCIAL BEHAVIOUR

Anti-social children and adolescents are vulnerable and active (often hyperactive or reactive).
They tend to have high aggression levels.
They tend to experience rejection in relationships with both parents and peers.
They generally produce low achievement scores.
They are likely to have a disposition which distinguishes them from others. Ultimately, when they become adults, they experience problematic relationships in the family, workplace and community.
Such children are defined in the literature as 'problematic children' or 'sensation-seeking adolescents'.
They have a need for high levels of arousal.
They tend to be impulsive.
They remain indifferent to regular punishment, requiring ever harsher means of punishment.
They lack the ability to react in a varied pattern, usually generating aggressive solutions for conflict situations.
They tend to underestimate the negative outcomes of their aggressive behaviour.
They experience negative relationships with peers, barring them from normal social learning acquired through peers.
They tend to spend time with other rejected children younger than them.
Anti-social children tend to socialize with peers who reinforce their anti-social behaviour. This is particularly relevant to aggressive children, who lack the ability to decrypt and interpret, and are thus overreactive towards others.
They tend to overestimate the degree of aggression directed towards them.
The siblings, like the rest of the family members, have characteristics of aggression.
From mid-childhood into adolescence, they are likely to engage in substance abuse.
They tend to exhibit promiscuity and delinquency.
Depression – manifested or latent – is common among such children.

THE ECO-SYSTEMIC APPROACH

In a previous book, Aldridge (1999) describes the process of becoming deviant as being a natural way of coping with change in a family organization. In any relationship, that relationship is stabilized into some form of regularity as an organized pattern. These patterns can be expressed as if they follow rules that prescribe and limit behaviour within a relational context. In this way relationships are organized into a relatively steady state. Individual and family behaviour is regulated by such rules, but because individuals and families need to change, these rules are not fixed; they are open to negotiation. Indeed, when such rules are fixed, and become inflexible, then perhaps we have the conditions for problem behaviour, and some problematic behaviour is an attempt to change the rules. Deviant behaviour in this sense is an extreme form of negotiation and has to be understood in a relational context.

Becoming deviant does not arise through the deliberate, knowing choice of the actor and it is essentially beyond his own control. In such a way, when children behave badly, it is not necessarily their fault, nor that of their parents. It is simply a way of trying to regulate relationships within the family and with the outside world, what we here call the ecology of family life that has gone wrong. For our purposes, this also means that we do not have to blame the deviant child nor the inadequate parents. We try our best but sometimes things go wrong.

Construing behaviour as deviant is a social and political process and deviance is the failure to obey group rules. However, it is an ambiguous state, as a person may belong to different groups with different rules. The same behaviour may be construed differently in different cultures and at different times; one culture's rebel may be another culture's innovator. This relativistic view emphasizes that the deviance is not the quality of the act, but a consequence of the act. Deviance becomes a political process involving the responses of other people to the behaviour. Giving meaning to behaviour and construing it as disruptive, and therefore challenging, is a political process of interpretation that must be negotiated after the act. This process is also at the core of all therapeutic encounters.

Deviance is required in social systems because it serves several important positive functions. Such behaviour is induced, if not arising spontaneously, sustained and regulated within a social context. Deviant behaviour in a family is a natural part of the role-differentiation process. Just as a family needs an emotional specialist, or an organizer, so it requires a deviant to change. We argue that there has to be a spectrum of behaviours from the deviant to the normal so that family members can occupy such necessary poles for the purpose of family change and cohesiveness.

The presence of deviant behaviour and accompanying sanctions serves an important purpose in defining normative boundaries. Deviant behaviour exemplifies the kinds of action which are not allowed, and sanctions show what will happen if such acts occur. Deviant acts and their accompanying sanctions provide concrete models for family rules. Only when a familial shared construing is present can interactions be smooth and predictable.

Families consistently apply sanctions to, but do not reject, a deviant member. Families seldom permanently stop deviant behaviour but maintain it at a level which promotes change. Once more the rate of change appears to be a critical variable. It is this notion of applying sanctions to but *not* rejecting the family member that is critical in considering disruptive children. As we know, isolation is a significant factor in the process of becoming suicidal (Aldridge 1999) and rejection plays its part in such isolation.

Every family group will define what constitutes deviance in its own way; for example, not working, drinking too much, being inappropriately sad, being noisy, bedwetting, sleeping a lot, wearing strange clothes, talking nonsense, not concentrating, not listening, answering back or working too hard. This depends upon an actively maintained set of rules and is a familial construing which each member knows. In this way individuals are informed by and inform such a construing: both personal and familial construings are interactive. Any behaviour may serve as evidence of deviance to maintain family viability.

The presence of a deviant person satisfies a certain need for predictability; by occupying one pole of a construct 'deviant' the other family members are allowed to occupy the pole of normality by contrasting themselves with the 'other' person. However, difficulties may arise when the family member who has broken norms in the past may also come to be the expected deviant member in the present. Mishler and Waxler (1966) point out that the child who is 'always different' is likely to be selected as the 'family's schizophrenic'. In another study (Wiggins, Dill and Schwartz 1965) the family member who is construed as 'weak' and 'different' will take on the role of deviant.

Deviant behaviour is a normal function in social systems which introduce necessary change to maintain stability. What is defined as deviant is based upon the context in which the behaviour occurs and, like any other extreme form of behaviour, this phenomenon is embedded in a wide social, cultural and political context of place and time. Episodes of disruptive behaviour belong to a cyclical pattern of escalating interactions. Many factors beyond the narrow confines of his family interact to impact on the child's life and development. This provides an understanding that the child's reality goes far beyond his family into society at large, suggesting a perspective of circular causality (see Figure 2.1).

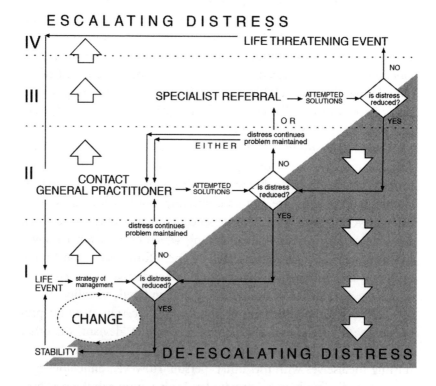

FIGURE 2.1 POSSIBLE CYCLES OF ESCALATING AND DE-ESCALATING DISTRESS (ALDRIDGE 1999)

New alternatives emerge out of this approach. The main advantage lies in redefining maladaptive delinquent acts as acts of attempted problem resolution thereby enhancing change. We can reframe *senseless acts of personal inadequacy* as *meaningful acts of social significance* and promote both change and conflict resolution. Conflict is neither the result of disagreements nor the result of failing relationships between two parties. Instead, conflict should be seen as a *description of the way in which the systemic behaviour is organized*. This helps us to negotiate conflict with everyone actively involved in a given situation.

This shift in focus has further implications, mainly for the goal of therapy. Therapy does not seek to fix what went wrong or to accommodate pathology and deviance – it enables the beginning of a process of change by referring to competence and resources. All efforts of all participants join to negotiate the same means and attain the same goal. Based on the effort to understand the rules, beliefs and language of the family, the therapist plays the role of a facilitator, offering choices and making them available to the family. Family boundaries not only provide the individual with his identity but also serve to constrain his behaviour.

The wider perspective of the eco-systemic approach has its focus not only on the deviant individual and his behaviour, but also on the whole complex of significant others and the different systems in which he operates. The emphasis on the collective, as well as the shift from feeling to action, is central to our alternative view of deviant and extreme behaviour where the person is located within close relationships that are themselves located within a larger context of community.

A MODEL OF THE SYSTEMIC MANAGEMENT OF DISTRESS

> Stabilization of relationship has been called the 'rule of the relationship' and works in the interest of economy (it leaves many behaviours from the repertoire to be used no longer). (Jackson 1965)

Behaviours are at once individual and collective, personal and social. They are also seen as either legitimate or illegitimate by individuals within the family, by the family itself and by their social context. Thus, particular personal behaviours may be legitimate to the child but illegitimate to the parents. Children think they are right in what they are doing. We as parents do not always agree.

From our perspective, challenging behaviour is seen as a strategy for controlling change and coping with stress within the family group. Families and small groups are stressed by developmental or life cycle changes where symptoms of illness may be used to reduce, manage, or avoid conflict. Challenging behaviour is a communicative process expressing a challenging situation that reflects the family system as a whole.

Families organize themselves to manage developmental crises in varying ways. Some families accommodate change easily and naturally without excess levels of distress. Some families develop within their own cultural tradition means of accommodating change that involves hostility and conflict leading to high levels of distress. In some families, overall familial distress is managed by one family member exhibiting symptoms. Effectively one person acts as a material cause representing distress at a different systemic level of interaction. The individual represents a pattern of social transactions.

Aldridge (1999) proposes a general model of the systemic management of distress. This model understands the management of systemic distress at different levels of organization: individual, familial or cultural (see Figures 2.1 and 2.2). Although conceived of as a circular process it will be necessary for the purpose of description to interrupt this circularity and begin at one point – we have to start somewhere. The point chosen to begin this cycle is that of a system facing a crisis.

In Figure 2.2 we see that (a) A developmental crisis is recognized by a system according to its own construings, that are in turn located within and informed by a cultural context. Something happens. A life event occurs. This event can be change in blood pressure, the entrance of a virus to the system or an argument between a child and a parent. Whatever it is, something happens that constitutes an 'event'. (b) As an adaptation to that event, thresholds of distress are threatened (see Section X in Figure 2.2). Someone is getting upset. (c) There then follows a strategic move to reduce that distress according to the repertoire of distress management that the individual has. Blood pressure may be regulated by sitting down and relaxing, the immune system may react to the virus or a child may cry for a while. Distress is reduced. What has happened is regulated successfully within the terms of the system itself. This means that: (d) distress is reduced, (e) the repertoire is validated – it works – and (f) stability is maintained. This is a simple homeostatic loop as we see in Section X of Figure 2.2.

However, should distress not be reduced then an alternative strategy (g) from the repertoire of distress management is used and the

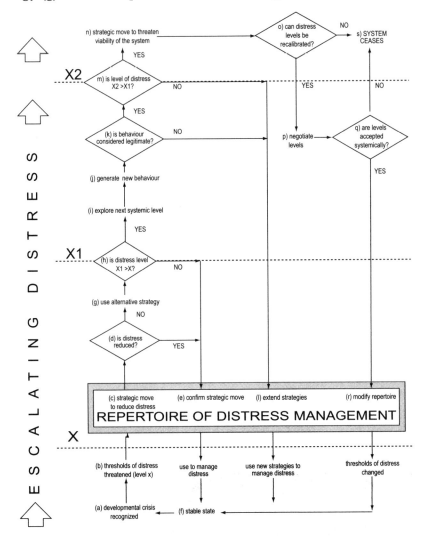

FIGURE 2.2 CHANGE AND A REPERTOIRE OF DISTRESS MANAGEMENT
(ALDRIDGE 1999)

system scrutinizes itself for levels of distress. We may reduce blood pressure by meditating, we can wait for a head cold to come and go or a child may run around boisterously and shout. If distress is reduced then this alternative strategy is validated as a legitimate means of reducing distress (e).

If distress continues to escalate to (h) where levels of distress are higher than in Section X, and systemic thresholds are threatened to excess to a point where the very viability of the system itself is threatened, then distress management strategies are explored from a higher level of systemic organization, stage (i) in Section X1. A shift occurs, from the organic to the personal, or from personal to marital, marital to familial, familial to communal, communal to social, or departmental to organizational. The child shouts, his mother cries, the father loses his temper.

At this stage the strategy will depend upon the systemic rules for distress management at this contextual level and will accord to the tradition of the system, that is the biography, memory and construing of the system. In this way 'new' behaviour to the individual is generated (j). Patients suffering emotional distress in contact with the psychiatric service are introduced to new ways of expressing that distress. Children and parents may learn from grandparents, social workers may suggest alternatives, religious elders may offer counselling, educational psychologists offer interventions.

If this behaviour is considered legitimate then it effectively extends the repertoire of distress management (l). Repertoires of distress are extended by being informed within a cultural matrix. We learn about the most sympathetic general practitioner, alternative medical practices, lay healing practices, differing psycho-therapeutic techniques, the latest diets, exercises and alternative lifestyles, to alleviate distress. It must be noted here that the current level of distress may be higher than at (b) although still within the thresholds of tolerable distress. In this way some systems live with raised levels of distress: learning to live with pain, anxiety, depression and delinquency. Indeed, some families live with a high level of conflict tolerance that may become accepted as everyday life.

At (m) current levels of distress may not fall to the initial levels. The system then calibrates itself to accommodate a higher level of distress. Distress at X2 is still greater than at X. When this occurs a family with a child who becomes symptomatic to maintain the family stability may become a family system with a necessarily symptomatic member, for example diabetic, asthmatic, problematic, anorectic, epileptic, tense, depressed or delinquent. Not only is the repertoire of distress management extended (l) but the initial thresholds of distress (b) are altered. The system returns itself to a stable state (f), but that state is altered. Conflict is endemic to the family system and becomes a way of relating.

If distress levels escalate to such an extent that systemic viability is further threatened, then (n) an overt strategic move is made to threaten the viability of the system. This move will be one which is culturally approved and based upon the systemic tradition of manifesting distress, for example blood sugar levels escalate into diabetes and then diabetic coma, essential hypertension becomes raised and develops into a stroke, delinquent behaviours escalate into challenging episodes of physical contact and abuse or strategies of medication escalate into self-poisoning. Someone may threaten to leave.

When a system becomes so threatened it will be necessary to implement measures to reduce distress and maintain systemic viability. This will be observed in those behavioural strategies used in a crisis. The vital question is whether thresholds of distress can be recalibrated (o). For some physiological levels this may not be physically possible and the patient dies. For some psychological levels, this calibration may mean a continuing psychotic episode or perpetual outbursts of anger. For some social situations there is withdrawal and temporary estrangement. Parents separate, or the child is taken into custody or lives elsewhere. Should these crisis strategies fail and the systemic thresholds be exceeded then the system will cease. Someone dies, leaves or is forcibly removed (s).

On the other hand, a crisis may successfully be negotiated and an attempt be made to recalibrate the systemic thresholds of distress (p) and change systemic construing (q). Thresholds of distress are then changed within the repertoire of distress management (r). Should the negotiation of such systemic change not be successfully validated throughout the system to the satisfaction of all members then the system will cease (s). In this way we see persons leave families through death, leave marriages through divorce, be expelled from school, sacked from an organization or discharged from hostels.

In this model, conflict can be seen as a means of promoting change and maintaining stability. Conflict may also promote further conflict and levels of distress may be tolerated at a level higher than the initial level. Conflict itself can become a life event threatening stability. Throughout the model, those strategic moves which attempt to reduce distress and recalibrate the system may act reflexively as 'life events' which in their turn are to be accommodated. This is the process of iatrogenesis; treatment can also be a cause of further problems. Similarly, the act of diagnosis, or the results of a test, are events that have ramifications. Being given the diagnosis of a disorder may be a relief to some parents in that the problem is located within the child and distress is managed by psychotropic medication. However, the repertoire of distress that utilizes medication may itself become a life event challenging the system. How these events are handled depends upon repertoires of distress management.

SOCIAL NETWORKS AND THE CONCEPT OF PERCEIVED SOCIAL SUPPORT

There is wide agreement among researchers on the importance of social support in the context of parenting. Social networks refer to significant others and social systems in which parents and their children interact – such as circles of relatives, friends or neighbours; or social circles formed through school, workplace or church. A wide net of social support will enable parents to resolve practical problems, supply emotional support on issues such as marital conflicts or problems at work, and assist parents in coping with a problematic child.

Social support influences the sense of certainty and self-esteem of the individual. This certainty is strongly connected to the individual's success in functioning in his various roles – among them his role as a parent. The findings of Flowers, Schneider and Ludtke (1996) attribute greater importance to perceived social support than to the actual supplied support the parent receives from his social network. Perceived social support expresses the parent's assurance of the availability of social support and its positive impact on him. The social network not only supplies emotional support but also validates the parent's belief in his own parental abilities. In the case of the problematic child, social support enhances positive acceptance of the child and moderates the parent's punitive reactions such as physical and verbal aggression, threats, rejection, nagging and criticism. A wide social network has a mutually positive impact on parents and their children.

PARENTAL COACHING

Parental coaching is designed to improve parental monitoring skills, steering parents clear of the inevitable failure associated with permissive, authoritarian or inconsistent parenting. The aim of parental coaching programmes is to empower the parent, by equipping him with appropriate parenting and coping skills. This is achieved by training him to balance restraint of the child's aggressive behaviour with gestures of love, affection and reconciliation towards the child that serve to expand the base of the relationship.

The focus is shifted away from the child's subversive behaviour and on to reinforcing positive behaviour and compliance through rewards; reducing punitive sanctions for negative behaviour and non-compliance to a necessary minimum; deciding which negative behaviours require response; deciding how immediate that response needs to be and formulating clear demands and requirements of the child.

These programmes emphasize positive reinforcement and shun criticism, claiming that this encourages the coercive child to draw closer to his parent. Most programmes involve some form of reward and punishment. Although they aim to reduce punishment to a minimum, they still sanction punitive measures for negative behaviour in general. Even the concept of 'time-out'[1] we perceive as a punitive measure. The problem with punitive measures is that they promote escalation between parents and children, especially at the adolescent stage (Bates, Pettit and Dodge 1995; Forehand and McMahon 1981).

The Non-Violent Resistance Model seeks to provide viable options to empower parents who are struggling with children who exhibit extreme behaviour.

---

1   'Time-out' is a measure whereby the parent sends the child to his room by himself after he has misbehaved. He is not allowed to leave his room until he has calmed down. Some suggest that the child should stay there for a specific duration of time.

HOW DOES THE NON-VIOLENT RESISTANCE MODEL DIFFER FROM OTHER MODELS?

The following equation emerges from the discussion of the various models that deal with a child exhibiting anti-social behaviour:

CHILD WITH A COERCIVE DISPOSITION
+ INEFFECTIVE PARENTING
+ ENVIRONMENT THAT ENHANCES INBORN PREDISPOSITIONS
= ANTI-SOCIAL BEHAVIOUR

However, this equation does not suggest how to put an end to the formative process of the anti-social behaviour.

THE INTENTION OF THE SUBJECT

Every attempt to describe anti-social behaviour considers the intention of the subject (i.e. the child). To determine whether an act is aggressive or not, one must take into account whether the intention of the subject is to consciously inflict harm (Bruyn and Raymann 1979). One problem highlighted in the literature is that the information about the subject – the child – always comes through a third party – those who interact with him: parents, other family members and teachers. As such, the information originates in subjective experience (Dishion *et al.* 1995; Kagan 1997; Spiker *et al.* 1992).

Since intervention in the proposed operative model of Non-Violent Resistance is directed towards the parent and not towards the child, the question regarding the intention of the subject becomes irrelevant. The parent is the ally in bringing about change, therefore the question regarding subjective reporting of the source of information on the subject (the child) becomes irrelevant as well. This neutral stance apportions no blame. We all try and accommodate change according to our personal and social resources. The stance taken here is that these resources, in our perspective, repertoires, are already resident in our social relationships. Rather than label a child deviant and the parents ineffective, we look at what can be done by the parents, that is, the when and how of parenting within a supportive milieu.

UNDERSTANDING BEHAVIOUR

The thesis presented here is that behaviour is not 'understood' when it is isolated from social systemic contexts. Deviant behaviour is often regarded as 'impulsive'. However, perhaps such behaviour only appears impulsive when regarded by an observer without a satisfactory theoretical understanding of such acts. Perhaps it is time to see how children and their parents make sense of what they do.

We use the term 'eco-system' in this book. 'Eco-system' is used here to refer to groups of related people and patterns of relationships. The emphasis is placed not only upon understanding elements in a system, that is the people involved, but also upon the relationships between those people, their shared meanings and values and the way they organize themselves. As such, it is a political reality, in the sense that the power is shared and divided and values are negotiated. Systems are located within bigger systems too, like Russian dolls, one within another. Thus we have the organ systems that compose the body, and various bodies that form a family, families that form a kinship network, networks that themselves form communities and communities that form nations. All together they are an eco-system. While this is of necessity materialistic as an example, what we propose is that there are such things as personal ideas that are related to a system of ideas within like-minded individuals that are related to particular eco-systems of ideas as cultural contexts. In this way we can speak not only of a biological or social ecology, but also of an ecology of ideas.

As individuals, with our own particular personal construings, we belong to communities of intimates with whom we are interdependent and with whom we share construings about how children should behave. Shared construings are negotiated in social interaction. Rather than being located within individuals these core constructs are located in the relationship, they are interactional rather than intrapsychic. It is these familial construings that define what a situation is, and give meaning to the external and internal events faced by a family. It is important to understand that these construings are negotiated in interaction and are not necessarily fixed for all time.

These construings will define what counts as a life event for a family and offer dimensions of seriousness, magnitude, legitimacy and content. Furthermore, within families we negotiate understandings of how episodes of conflict are to be punctuated into events, beginnings and endings. The location of events in terms of punctuation and magnitude, content and legitimacy are contextualized further by considerations of accountability, duty and competence. In this way, constructs are combined into a rules-based understanding of inter-action. These rules of ordering meaning and action are negotiated, argued, stretched and ignored in the political interaction between intimate others. These too are our moral perspective on behaviour.

In this way, no normative inter-relational order is specified but it must continually be constituted and regulated. This order does not reside in individuals but in the relationship between persons, nor is this orderliness binding and indefinite but continually negotiated. What appears to be stable is rather a state of negotiated stability with a negotiated agreement about what counts as change and how that change can remain stable. This does not preclude individuals from having personal construings of reality which are negotiated within other social contexts, nor are these contexts separate. It is perhaps the negotiation of social construings in other social contexts – that is, at work, at school, with friends, with lovers – that introduce change into the family context.

Taking these two ideas together, we can follow the family rules hypothesis of Aldridge (Aldridge 1999). This hypothesis proposes that any relationship stabilizes itself into some form of regularity and organized pattern. These relational regularities, or patterns, can be expressed as if they follow rules that prescribe and limit behaviour within a relational context. In this way relationships are organized into a relatively steady state. Individual and family behaviour is regulated by such rules, but because individuals and families need to change, these rules are not fixed; they are open to negotiation. Indeed, when such rules are fixed, and become inflexible, then perhaps we have the ground for problem behaviour, and some problem behaviour is an attempt to change the rules. Deviant behaviour in this sense is an extreme form of negotiation and has to be understood in a relational context. Challenging child behaviour then can be seen as an extreme form of negotiation within a relational system. What we need is a model that offers alternative construings and a forum for negotiation.

CHAPTER THREE

The Non-Violent Resistance Model

The Non-Violent Resistance Model, as a theoretical and practical alternative, does not attempt to change the child. Instead, it seeks to alter and modify the actions, reactions and interactions of the child's immediate environment. We are an active part of that environment. We provide the necessary ecology for behaviour to thrive. The Non-Violent Resistance Model presumes that it is necessary, even obligatory, to build effective non-violent barriers to confront a child's destructive behaviour as well as to restore authority to the parents.

The Non-Violent Resistance Model considers the following questions of prime importance:

- Where and how is negative emotion turned into negative action? To put it another way, when is aggression translated into extreme behaviour?

- In which physical or virtual environment does this emotional and cognitive translation take place and what furnishes those environments?

- What type of message (or lack of message) influences the child's inhibition?

According to the operative model of Non-Violent Resistance, the parent recognizes that as the child's care-taker, his child's welfare is the primary consideration in all his actions. His actions towards altering his child's anti-social behaviour are independent of his child's agreement, and most importantly, independent of the anticipated outcome.

The plan of action initiated by the parent must continue even when it is unsuccessful in promoting the anticipated change within the child. As Gandhi said, 'We have always control over the means and never the ends' (Bruyn and Rayman 1979, p.6).

In this sense the parent's intentions are not to bring about submission of the child, not to triumph over the child, but to change his own condition as a parent. This change of condition must be the parent's primary motivation for action. From this standpoint, parental action is directed toward the child, yet not dependent on the child, neither on his agreement to it nor on his co-operation with it. The parent's main objective is to develop and establish a new order in the home, which will enable him as a parent to develop vital resources such as self-reliance and self-governance.

By encouraging these attributes, The Non-Violent Resistance Model seeks to promote a progression of change and healing. However, this change hinges upon the parent's ability to recognize and utilize his moral rights and obligations as a parent. To achieve and nurture change, we need the following ideas:

- Give up the pretence of changing the other, in this case the child.

- Take responsibility only for our own actions.

- Agreed initiatives must be carried out regardless of estimated probability of success.

- The child's agreement to the initiative is not mandatory for change to occur.

CONFLICTS AND ESCALATION

The threatening dynamic of a coercive child and helpless parent ultimately creates a rigid interpersonal system. In this ongoing process of conflict and intimidation, the parent loses sight of the possibility of different, more productive types of interaction with his child.

Several factors contribute to the preservation of mutual or complementary escalating conditions. There is a *tendency to dominance*: a parent and/or a child who thinks 'Who is the more powerful boss?' is likely to intensify escalation. The potential for escalation rises with the level of *emotional arousal* of the parties in conflict. As the conflict continues, *communication* becomes rigid, revolving mainly around matters of conflict. In many cases, communication is severed completely. This narrowing phenomenon encourages and amplifies escalation, preventing the parties from seeking alternatives for resolution.

The Non-Violent Resistance Model presumes that a dual process of escalation occurs in almost every incidence of children's violent and extreme behaviour. These intertwined processes feed and reinforce one another. Hostility escalates and this hostility breeds further hostility. In terms of a repertoire of management, this becomes limited to a restricted set of responses of hostility and submission that all the involved parties share. As parents submit, the child steps up his demands and his aggression.

Parents may respond in one of two ways:

- In kind – forcefully, in the same tenor as his child – with screams, curses, threats, severe punishments or slapping. The child's counter-response is then even more extreme.

- Submission – when facing a belligerent coercive child who is screaming, threatening, cursing, humiliating, and inflicting pain, ultimately the parent prefers to simply submit. The child deduces that he can in the future employ these means towards achieving his end. Weakness of a submissive parent sets into motion a merry-go-round where the parent's frustration intensifies and with it the child's tendency towards further explosions.

Identifying this process of dual escalation is critical in dealing with violent behaviour. After it has been identified, the principles of the operative Non-Violent Resistance Model can be implemented.

THE SOCIO-POLITICAL ORIGINS OF THE NON-VIOLENT RESISTANCE MODEL

Non-Violent Resistance is an ideology that originated in the realm of socio-political conflict. This ideology provided a means for ethnic groups to confront the oppression and tyranny wielded against them by their governments. The movement's most notable advocates were Gandhi and Martin Luther King. Despite the severity of the conflict in both these struggles, the main actors did not use violence against the governing powers nor capitulate to them. In both these struggles, that were steeped in serious conflict, much effort went into designing a plan of action that would realize their desired goals without either being drawn into confrontational violence nor submitting.

The abysmal failure of attempts at verbal persuasion on the one hand, coupled with moral and ideological considerations discouraging violence, made Non-Violent Resistance the strategy of choice among victims of political and social oppression. Along with those considerations were practical considerations, the other side being more powerful and having more resources to inflict violence. Non-violence, however, could attain the desired goals with limited loss and fewer casualties.

THE CONCEPT OF CONFLICT AND NON-VIOLENT ACTION

The concepts of absence of violence and creative conflict are germane to the Non-Violent Resistance ideology. Neither Gandhi nor Luther King had the intention of conquering their opponents or subjugating them. Instead they sought to uncover the truth behind the conflict – to understand the underlying reasons behind the violent outcome. If and when possible, they sought to win the understanding and friendship of their opponents.

Non-Violent Resistance staunchly opposed passivity, perceiving it as a primary cause for violence. Instead Non-Violent Resistance established as a supreme value the search for a solid understanding of the truth on the one hand and the establishment of an active sense of respect towards the opponents on the other hand. The ultimate goal for the Non-Violent Resistance proponent is to be free of fear, rejection and vindictiveness. This type of intention challenges the traditional definition of conflict that is based on the perception of a struggle between two sides to overcome one another (Bruyn and Rayman 1979; Charney 1978).

To summarize, there are three factors that distinguish Non-Violent Resistance's concept of conflict from the conventional concept of conflict and conflict resolution:

- refusal to use physical force against opponents
- conscious and meditated intention not to overpower the opponents

- endeavouring and taking measures to act against the causes of violence at the same time as transforming patterns of domination.

Three central principles that direct the plan of action of Non-Violent Resistance are adapted to the Non-Violent Resistance Model:

- the categorical abstention from violence on the one hand

- the recognition that the struggle is necessary on the other hand

- the emphasis on the singular significance of free will as the agent of change in patterns of obedience (Sharp 1973).

PARENTAL AUTHORITY AND PRESENCE

As in the case of socio-political obedience, first one must define the sources that promote a state of obedience. Just as those factors can be strengthened or weakened in the socio-political realm, they can be equally strengthened or weakened in the family realm. The Non-Violent Resistance Model attempts to define the sources of parental helplessness, proposing methods of sapping them of their strength in order to achieve the ultimate goal of restoring parental authority to its rightful place. (For elaboration on the model and its practical implications see Chapter 10.)

The absence or loss of a parental figure, even at a later stage in a child's life, has been known to cast a long shadow on that child's growth and development. Along with this tangible loss, there is an awakening realization of another type of loss that is becoming increasingly widespread amongst families today. In spite of physical presence, the child is increasingly experiencing the parental figure as absent (Omer 2000, 2001). A parent whose ability to act is neutralized, whose personal voice is silenced, is for all intents and purposes absent in the life of his child.

Contrary to common opinion, parental authority is not 'given' by the coercive, violent child to his parents; submission is a choice that parents make. Even the direst of sanctions need not force a state of obedience. The authority of a parent is not in the child's hands, it is entirely up to the parent to assume his rightful role. However, when a parent is faced with a child beyond his control, he is overcome by a combination of compassion, pity, guilt and fear which become both the motor and the impediment in his mode of action (Bandura 1969; Cavell 2001; Patterson *et al.* 1992). And so the question remains: how can a parent habituated into obedience make the difficult shift from obedience to autonomy?

The operative model offered here strives to first rehabilitate and then empower the parental voice to the point that a parent is capable of saying to his child, 'I am here! I am not giving up on you, and I am not giving in to you!' The model is based on the premise that even in the most submissive person there is a parallel voice, however weak, that must be located and recruited towards this mission.

THE PROPERTIES OF NON-VIOLENT PARENTAL ACTION

The properties of non-violent parental action are:

- Courageous and unwavering stand on central issues, where all the parent's capabilities and resources are mobilized towards frustrating the child's destructive challenges.

- Absolute rejection of verbal or physical violence against the child such as: hitting, cursing, threatening and humiliating.

- Resolute stance of determined struggle against violence and destructive behaviour on the one hand, coupled with a demonstrated respect for the child on the other. Attempting to find a solution in which the child will not feel humiliated or defeated.

- Exhibiting a readiness to absorb and remain firm in the course of a conflict (without capitulating to the child's demands), thereby maintaining calm and allowing the parents to regroup.

- Offering ongoing gestures of reconciliation that are not in any way conditional on the child's behaviour or positive change.

Non-violent parental action relies on three important principles (see Figure 3.1).

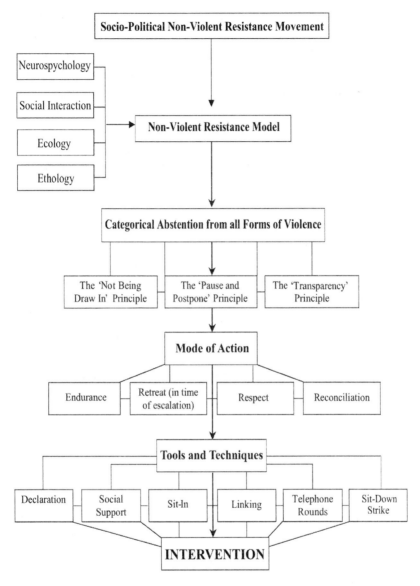

FIGURE 3.1. FLOW CHART OF THE INTERVENTION ACCORDING TO THE
NON-VIOLENT RESISTANCE MODEL: FROM THEORY TO INTERVENTION

1. The principle of 'not being drawn in'

There is a mechanical automatic quality that characterizes repeated
entry into states of confrontation. These states escalate rapidly, taking

on a dynamic of their own. Those parents who are at greatest risk of being drawn in to repeated confrontation with their children are ones who talk, preach, persuade, rebuke, apologize, argue, threaten, yell and promise compensation. According to the Non-Violent Resistance Model, these responses are yet one more form of being drawn in to conflict. Parents must avoid being drawn in to unnecessary confrontations by identifying the triggers which set them off, raising their own self-awareness and guarding themselves vigilantly against succumbing to the child's provocation (Eisenberg and Murphy 1995; Patterson *et al.* 1984).

2. The 'pause and postpone' principle
Changing the basic conditions of violence is a function of meditated and measured response. This principle is based on the rationale that a response must follow only after thorough and deliberate evaluation and preparation – postponing gives the parents enough breathing space to form a pre-meditated response. A rushed, impulsive, knee-jerk reaction – like that of the child – is a recurring pitfall for parents.

3. The 'transparency' principle: removing the cloak of secrecy
Giving a public face to the struggle is based on the following axioms:

- To break out of isolation is the first step to breaking free of violence.

- Maintaining secrecy preserves and perpetuates the continuum of violence, allowing the perpetrator to continue unchecked.

- Maintaining secrecy prevents the parties from entertaining alternatives other than giving up or reacting with harsher retribution.

- The determination and endurance that the struggle demands will be greatly enhanced through the support and solidarity of the wide collective.

- Breaking out of isolation allows for the inclusion of a third party who can exercise his influence over the aggressive/coercive child (Cairns *et al.* 1994; Fisher, Ury and Paton 1981).

Removing the veil of secrecy from the child's violent behaviour — through the declaration (see Chapter 10) and by mobilizing outside support — serves to foster a new confidence within the parents and a renewed hope in the process. This newfound confidence can profoundly impact on the child, manifesting itself in a decrease in the severity and incidence of his violent eruptions.

SUMMARY

The operative Non-Violent Resistance Model assumes that the success of the Non-Violent Resistance Model initiative will be related to the degree to which the parents are able to curb their child's coercion tactics and can extricate themselves from their previous patterns of obedience and co-operation within the parent–aggressive child relationship. It is also necessary that parents are convinced of the morality of the goal towards which they are working, that is, removing violence from the home and restoring parental authority. The consequence of this is a steadiness and consistency of strategy and tactics employed to actualize the struggle. Parents are encouraged not to flip from one strategy or tactic to another. Parents need to develop the ability to set reasonable achievable goals for themselves, as well as make reasonable achievable demands of their child, without backing down. Similarly, parents have to be committed to the required self-restraint to execute the plan successfully. To achieve this, parents will need to exhibit unity regardless of other problematic interpersonal issues and exercise patience, perseverance and endurance.

A first step is for parents to break the secrecy surrounding the problem and maintain transparency about the situation in their home. This means that parents must show a willingness to involve others and enlist their support network in this process.

The operative model of Non-Violent Resistance goes to great lengths to prepare tools and tactics to implement the goal of restoring the status of the parent as an authority figure in the home. It provides strategies to activate personal presence; presents tactics to prevent violence between siblings; recruits outside support; wields the pressure of 'public opinion' against the violent behaviour patterns of the child; allows parents access to those settings in which the child behaves destructively which were taboo until now; forms relationships with the 'who's who' in the child's life in order to win their support in resisting the child's destructive tendencies; and hones methods of supervision that diminish the child's access to the hideouts to which he might escape in order to act out his destructive intentions (see Chapter 10).

The Non-Violent Resistance Model assures the firm moral and practical support required to successfully implement this plan of action. Furthermore, it clearly enunciates a therapeutic attitude that morally encourages, and practically instructs, parents to move from a passive state of acceptance and resignation to an active state of implementing essential change and transformation.

We will see in the following case study chapters that the therapeutic intervention takes place over a short period of time. The basis of such a therapeutic approach is not to engage in a massive reappraisal of the family system but to initiate enough change in the right direction – to get the family moving in a direction that satisfies their own needs adequately. This approach is analogous to helping a careful driver who has driven off the road in winter. We cannot change the climate so that winters never occur, nor can we accompany him using another vehicle to his journey's end but giving him enough purchase to get out of the snow, back onto the road and get going will suffice so that he can carry on independently.

In Aldridge's earlier studies (1999), we saw how the very act of questioning families about their ways to resolve problems, enlisting their expertise rather than using external expert solutions, was efficacious. The same therapeutic stance is taken here. Similarly, Aldridge also discovered that the process of careful questioning about what happened and when, encouraged families to take a different stance on the problem; rather than placing blame on an individual, the emphasis is shifted to analysing sequences of interaction and developing repertoires of problem-solving solutions.

CHAPTER FOUR

From Theory to Practice: The Intervention

How does one get from the theory of the Non-Violent Resistance Model to implementing it in a full-scale intervention? In this chapter we will bridge the gap between the theory of the Non-Violent Resistance Model and how we implemented it in practice, in our intervention. After describing the implementation in this chapter, we will proceed to add further meaning and real-life applicability in the ensuing chapters, through six lively case studies garnered from the intervention.

Aldridge's concept of an eco-systemic management of distress is one of the main foundations on which the Non-Violent Resistance Model operates. Conflict resolution is negotiating conflict through a shared, focused effort of all participants in a given situation. We see this in the way that parents and other family members, including significant others in the community, negotiate solutions to the problem.

There is an extended repertoire of behaviours for the management of distress in families. Challenging behaviour is seen as a strategy for controlling change and coping with stress within the family group. Families or small groups are stressed by developmental or life cycle changes, where symptoms of illness may be used to reduce, manage, or avoid conflict. Challenging behaviour is a communicative process expressing a challenging situation that reflects the family system as a whole. Families organize themselves to manage developmental crises in varying ways. Some families accommodate change easily and naturally without excess levels of distress. Some families develop within their own cultural tradition a means of accommodating change that involves hostility and conflict leading to high levels of distress. In the families in these studies, familial distress is exhibited as symptoms by the child.

THE INTERVENTION: THE RESULTS OF THE STUDY

Based on the moral principles of the Non-Violent Resistance Model, and its eco-systemic approach, the Non-Violent Resistance Model short-term intervention seeks to mobilize change in the perpetuated cycles of escalatory parent–child relationships. It is designed to restore the parent's voice and responsibilities and to restore the privileges and opportunities inherent in the parent–child relationship. The three studies (for detailed presentation of procedure and results of the studies, see Avraham-Krehwinkel 2005) are targeted at parents of children with severe disruptive behaviours to enable them to gain control over escalatory exchanges with their child and to build up their parental presence.

Our preliminary work aimed to qualitatively examine the effect of the intervention and check the utilization of the *Guidebook for Parents*[1] – the pilot work with which the first ten families began. In this initial stage, the parents reported three clear outcomes:

- a reduction in escalatory incidents with the child in question and within the family as well
- a reduced sense of parental helplessness
- an increased sense of parental self-efficacy.

All of the families who had begun the intervention concluded it as expected.

In the second stage, we confirmed our hypotheses that according to the operative model of Non-Violent Resistance the intervention effects change within the parents' behaviour and self-perception, as well as in the level of escalation of parent and child. There was:

- a decrease in authoritarian parental discipline style
- a decrease in parental sense of helplessness

---

1 The original *Guidebook for Parents* used in this phase of the intervention was expanded and is featured in Chapter 10.

- a decrease in the level of escalatory behaviour of parent and child alike
- maintenance of affection levels in spite of the difficulties
- an increase in adequacy of support
- evident gender differences along all the examined variables.

Once again, all families who began the intervention remained until completion.

Our final study was designed to examine whether the results of the second study could be replicated to establish the viability of the Non-Violent Resistance intervention and its techniques to initiate the targeted change. This time it was designed to meet stricter criteria for evidence-based research. The experimental design compared an immediate group (ten families) who underwent the intervention, with a suspended group, who awaited the intervention (12 families).

The third study yielded significant results:

- a decrease in parents' sense of helplessness
- a decrease in authoritarian and permissive discipline styles
- a decrease in the level of escalatory behaviour of parent and child alike
- maintenance of affection levels in spite of the difficulties
- an increase in adequacy of support
- evident gender differences along all the examined variables.

The intervention increased parental ability to mobilize and gain support enabling them to adequately address their child's problematic behaviour. The parents' new sense of power and self-efficacy was attributed to their own newfound capability. Progress was seen as being achieved through the families' own internal resources. Female participants clearly derived more benefit from the intervention than male participants through all the different measurements.

In this study, distress was reduced. A new set of behavioural strategies was included within the repertoire of distress management. Higher levels of distress were not maintained. Conflict was seen as an attempt to promote change and maintain family viability. From some perspectives, we may describe 'misbehaving' as attempting to involve a 'distant' father in a difficult marital relationship nested in a stressful community in an uncaring society. These perspectives pathologize the actors involved. What we attempt to do is to neutralize such negativity, ask what happens and seek those resources that are available. Change happens, we have the resources to adapt, and we are responsible for developing those resources within communities. Significantly by extending our repertoires of behaviour we promote the mutual acceptance of legitimacy, and this is tolerance.

IN PRACTICE: CASE STUDIES

In Chapters 5 to 8, we demonstrate how the model is translated into practical therapy. Attempts to explain, discuss, convince, argue, preach, threaten or withdraw are present in any confrontation. The confrontation usually escalates the more such means are used and abused. Such confrontations usually evoke a sequence of responses from the parents, ranging from anger that serves to amplify the confrontation, all the way to despair and helplessness that lead to giving in and giving up. This is the process of family politics. The process of escalating behaviours is an attempt to coerce, manipulate, validate, communicate or negotiate some mutual goal whereby persons do something differently together. It is a political act with a small 'p'. In this process, the original relational nexus becomes disturbed and one person becomes threatened with isolation, alienation or banishment.

The parents' response is usually based on the widespread belief that it is essential to respond immediately to any argument or provocation coming from the child. The principle of 'not being drawn in' depends on the principle of postponed response. Both principles are based on not reacting directly to the confrontation or the attempts to lead to one. Instead, the parent reacts after carefully considering the appropriate response and exercising it at the point where both the parent and the child are no longer in an agitated and confrontational state.

Attempts to coerce are bound to fail because:

- The nature of the escalation is such that each party tends to entrench itself in its position, leading to a situation where neither side is capable of listening to the other.

- Children with oppositional traits are interested in the argumentation process itself, while adults usually concentrate on achieving some outcome from the discussion. For the child, conflict is the relationship. For the parents, arguing is meant to achieve a resolution to conflict but the parental relationship is to remain.

What we ask of the parents then is to remain steadfast in their approach and provide a holding environment for the child.

According to the operative Model of Non-Violent Resistance, the well-being of an individual is a product of his being networked in supportive relationships both within and outside his family, and of his interactions within this network. The more connections he cultivates with his surroundings, the more stable is his movement within his network. As such, the network echoes and resonates with the presence of that individual. Each of these connections serves as an additional outline that defines the individual's presence and being.

The intervention consists of four basic stages, each with its objectives:

Stage I: Setting the goals of the intervention

Stage II: Identifying escalatory dynamics, reasoning and reframing

Stage III: Returning the pyramid to its natural state

Stage IV: Establishing a network of support

Last Session: Embedding parent–child–family relations within the larger context of the social network

For each of the cases presented here, we see a pattern of relationship generating a specific challenge that appears frequently in therapy. Together, they show that by adhering to the principles of the model, an old pattern is replaced by a new one. The cases will be presented in detail to show the reader the process in its making. The last two cases present a special challenge. They show clearly how fractures in the family network and loose contacts with the community breed dissonance, distress and dysfunction on different planes of family management, as well as within each of its members.

CHAPTER FIVE

A Young Child with Self-Destructive Behaviour

Mr and Ms Schmidt are in their late thirties and both have secondary education. They have three children – Jennifer is ten, Eddie is eight and Thomas is six years old. The mother is a native German while the father emigrated from France to Germany about 15 years ago. The father appears to be strongly attached to his native culture and does not have a very good command of German. Both parents work in marketing and are away from home until the late afternoon or evening. The family resides in a rented house in a rural community.

The referral for therapy was initiated by Ms Schmidt, who provided a list of severe behavioural problems of her younger child Thomas: outbursts of violence at home and in the nursery and a total refusal to be disciplined, especially when the father was involved. In addition, each exchange or argument culminated in alarming self-destructive and suicidal exclamations from Thomas.

In her initial description, Ms Schmidt emphasized the father as being 'irrelevant' to the therapy since he only takes a peripheral role in Thomas's life, is often absent until late in the evening and any of his attempts to communicate with Thomas end up in a 'disaster'. The father corroborated this view at the intake meeting.

THE INTAKE SESSION: A HISTORY OF TRAUMA

At the meeting, the parents begin by describing an incident that occurred at the nursery when Thomas was two years old. Thomas suffered first degree burns when the teacher spilled a bowl of boiling hot soup down the front of him. The ensuing hospitalization and recurring prolonged treatment was the cause for motor difficulties, stuttering and behavioural problems both at home and in the nursery. Since the accident, Thomas has become aggressive and any frustration he experiences results in a tantrum. In his contact with other children he has adopted aggressive behaviour, beating them and destroying toys and other objects.

The parents sued the nursery but, in effect, ended up suing the community, as the nursery was run by the community. The parents claimed that in order to protect themselves and the community's interests, the nursery kept much of Thomas's behaviour subsequent to the accident from the parents, and neglected to notify them of the change and the severity of his behaviour. The parents found themselves isolated and left the community when the situation became unbearable. Once Thomas started attending the nursery in the new residence, complaints and reports concerning his problematic behaviour alerted them, resulting in the referral to therapy.

Since the accident, and during Thomas's long rehabilitation period, a structural change took place in the family, resulting in the creation of two camps. The mother, who was unemployed at the time, looked after Thomas and dedicated her time to him entirely. The father, on the other hand, dedicated the little time remaining after work to the other children. At the point of referral, which is four years after the accident, the two camps appear to have established themselves and cemented the feeling of separation between them.

Ms Schmidt has close ties with her parents' family and has two very close female friends who know nothing of the problematic behaviour of Thomas either at the nursery or at home. Mr Schmidt emphasizes that he has no social contacts or friends outside his wife and her family.

Both parents agree that the main burden falls on Ms Schmidt's shoulders, in spite of the fact that she works till 5pm every day. She returns home tired and, during the limited time she has with Thomas, has to put up with his outbursts and aggressive behaviour. She often comes up with expressions such as: 'I can't listen to him anymore,' 'I no longer respond to him' and 'I am disengaging.' She expresses restrained anger at the father's inability to take a more active role in the house. She keeps emphasizing that since she knows she cannot expect any more help or involvement, she has stopped asking for it and has resigned herself to doing everything herself: 'By the time I explain what I want him to do, and by the time he grasps what has to be done, I manage to do it myself.'

The father responds by saying that his wife does what needs to be done far better than he can. According to him, having grown up under a strict and authoritarian father who exercised severe mental and physical pressure on him, he consciously avoids any conduct that may make him seem dictatorial, preferring his wife to do the disciplining of the kids. He adds that he finds it difficult to interact with Thomas saying that he 'does not have anything in common with him' and that 'nothing seems to interest him' and 'I do not know how to arouse his interest in anything.' The interactions with his other children are much easier and smoother and revolve mainly around sports.

The parents complain of endless arguments with Thomas that inevitably result in anger and their withdrawal from him. Both claim that 'there is not a moment of peace in the house'. The mother says that she is 'always on alert for the next explosion to happen', and the father adds 'I feel as if I am walking on eggs and that I have to watch out what I do or say the whole time.'

At home, any attempts by the father to assert any authority are rejected completely by Thomas and any request or demand from the father is simply ignored. When attempting to discipline Thomas, the father sometimes resorts to threatening him, causing Thomas to respond aggressively and provocatively: 'Who are you anyway?' and 'What can you do anyway?' and 'Well, I dare you to do something to me!'

Mornings provide a rich source of confrontation which rapidly escalates to outbursts of shouting and threatening. As the parents are under immense pressure to get to work, they sometimes resort to literally 'dragging' Thomas half dressed to the nursery. At home as in the nursery, Thomas is only capable of concentrating on a game or a task for short periods. At home, he tends to disturb his siblings and often provokes them to the point where shouting and beatings follow. They 'cannot cross each others' path without hurting each other' is how the situation is summed up by the parents.

The nursery teacher describes Thomas as an impulsive kid with a short fuse, who cries easily, is devoid of any sense of danger and has a tendency to hurt himself. Both the parents and the nursery staff describe him as someone who trespasses physical boundaries in his wish to express warmth and love. He hugs and kisses other kids against their will. The mother tells of a neighbour who complained of Thomas trying to forcefully kiss her daughter. Thomas attempts the same with adults and demands repeated signs of fondness from the nursery teacher and staff. The mother also discloses that at the local swimming pool, Thomas developed a habit of pinching ladies' bottoms.

Helplessness and detachment

Any attempt to rein in Thomas's bouts of aggression are counteracted by violent responses, sometimes resulting in Thomas banging his head against a wall shouting 'I don't want to live anymore,' 'I deserve to die,' 'I am a bad boy,' or 'I deserve punishment' and 'Hit me.' This pattern of behaviour is repeated at the nursery and at home, causing adults and in particular the parents to feel, as Ms Schmidt puts it 'in a state of total paralysis'. The parents oscillate between no response at all and an aggressive response that includes shouting at him, shaking him, pushing and slapping him in the face. In fact, Thomas has not only become the 'Terror of the nursery' but also the 'Horror of the house', deepening the social isolation that his family finds itself in and causing them to avoid being seen in public with him altogether.

In terms of their presence, it can be argued that the Schmidt parents have been pushed to the periphery both in social terms and as being relevant to Thomas. Each parent retreats into a form of seclusion by exercising different forms of detachment from Thomas and their social surroundings. The mother tends to break this disengagement through outbursts of authority-imposing measures and anger; she then retreats back into the former state of disengagement. The father plays a peripheral role due to his inability to engage with his surroundings and especially with his child Thomas. He gives up on interacting with Thomas since he regards such interactions as doomed to failure. Furthermore, he is perceived as playing a peripheral role by his wife who defines him as 'irrelevant'. Within the pattern of interaction between the parents, the father is pushed aside by his wife's desire to be fast and efficient and as a result of her lack of trust in his ability to carry out what is needed for Thomas.

The sources of parental weakness of the socially isolated Schmidt parents are amplified by:

- A feeling of shame and a desire to keep Thomas's behavioural problems a secret.

- The father's sense of detachment from his surroundings. Put in his own words when asked about his social connections: 'Don't ask me; I am not a human being; ask my wife.'

- The feeling of being socially alienated from the community as a result of the lawsuit against the nursery. Even in their new community they are regarded as outsiders.

Such factors feed on each other, amplifying the sense of helplessness and weakness of the parents, between themselves, their surroundings and mostly between themselves and their child.

The endless spiral

It is easy to identify the endless spiral that starts by giving in to Thomas's demands from fear of what he might say and do. Giving in, however, not only strengthens Thomas's demands and his reactions to his frustration, but also deepens his parents' feeling of anger and despair. The parents' refuge in a form of disengagement can be easily understood when considering this spiral. This, in return, only increases Thomas's efforts to draw his parents' attention to himself. These efforts feed the parents' guilt feelings and in turn amplify their anger and despair. The switch from a heated and lengthy exchange of words to disengagement, similar to the switch from an anger outburst to capitulation, leaves the parents with a deepening feeling of weakness and helplessness.

At the end of the intake meeting, several conclusions are formed: The aim of the treatment is to:

- clarify to the parents that the behaviour in the nursery and at home are the result of the same underlying problem

- help the parents to break out of their disengagement and reassert themselves as central figures in Thomas's life

- break the parents' isolation by strengthening the understanding and mutual support between them
- improve the links with their surroundings in order to gain the support of neighbours and friends.

Such understanding is aimed to support the parents in:

- detecting and controlling the process of escalation during encounters with Thomas
- taking a firm, consistent and non-violent stand against Thomas's self-destructive and suicidal exclamations
- containing and calming Thomas down in moments of crisis without breaking down and disengaging from him.

THE FIRST SESSION: CHALLENGING OLD PATTERNS

The parents return to the first meeting after reading the relevant sections of the *Guidebook for Parents* given to them earlier. This meeting lays the foundation that should serve the parents to identify situations that are likely to result in escalation, how to avoid being dragged into them, how to contain them through direct, clear and unambiguous messages, and how to avoid confusion between such direct interaction and arbitrary commands. Emphasis on these points is a recurring theme in meetings and telephone conversations in the weeks to come.

New regulation

Both parents bring up examples of situations where they find it difficult to convey a clear message without falling into the trap of wordy and lengthy discussions (the father) or military-style commands (the mother). In this meeting, the parents are instructed to change their mode of interaction with Thomas. The mother is encouraged to avoid wordy, preaching, cajoling or threatening exchanges. In addition, she is asked to refrain from wordy exchanges and instead give clear, explicit orders. Both parents are recommended to use direct and focused speech, with a quiet tone and with an unambiguous message. At this point, the father's difficulty in understanding what is being asked becomes clear and he repeatedly expresses his worry that a direct and unambiguous style of interaction will be perceived by Thomas as authoritarian commands. According to him, it is sufficient that his wife does so and that he will not be able to carry it out. He recounts the traumatic experience of his authoritarian father that he still carries with him, stating that in the little time that he has to spend with his kids, he does not wish to exercise his power and command them.

At this meeting, new sleeping and waking up routines are agreed on in which Thomas will wake up half an hour earlier than usual. This additional time will be used to pamper him. On the mornings when the father is responsible for bringing him to the nursery, the mother is asked to phone Thomas before he leaves the house and wish him a pleasant journey to the nursery with his father. The father is expected to do likewise on days when the mother is responsible for getting Thomas to the nursery.

Because of Thomas's attention deficit, the parents are asked to regulate his activities on his return from the nursery and create a structured routine. Such a routine is aimed at making his afternoons and evenings less pressurized. The routine is expected to allocate appropriate and measured periods for watching TV and playing with the computer; such activities invariably became a focus of argument in the past. The routine is expected to leave time for 'fun and leisure' inactivity – pampering, joking, playing – activities that require full concentration and emotional attention from the mother.

At the end, the team brings up the idea of recruiting support. The parents and especially the father react uncomfortably to the suggestion and express fear of the possible exposure that such a request would inevitably lead to. The team assures the parents that it is far easier than they anticipate. They are asked to consult the *Guidebook for Parents* and to adhere to the points agreed at the meeting. The team promises to discuss it at the next meeting.

THE SECOND SESSION: CONFRONTING PERSISTENCE

At this meeting, the parents report on trying to implement all the recommendations from the previous meetings. In spite of carrying them out, it appears that Thomas persists in his old ways.

The discussion goes back to the new definition of the unclear and diffuse manner in which the parents and the nursery team interact with Thomas, resulting from their helplessness and paralysis when confronted with Thomas's self-destructive and suicidal exclamations.

The team draws the parents' attention to the view that Thomas's self-destructive talk feeds from the same weakness in which the adult world finds itself, and that this weakness amplifies Thomas's outbursts. A brain-storming session of the therapy team and the parents interprets Thomas's self-destructive talk as a desperate attempt to test the parents' and nursery team's presence and their determination to stay the course with him. This new understanding that each self-destructive utterance from Thomas is a way of testing how far he can push his parents, or how much the care-takers can take without breaking, opens an opportunity for change. In other words, it enables the adult world, including parents and care-takers, to shift from helplessness, fear and paralysis to a forceful resistance to Thomas's self-destructive exclamations, without relinquishing control. This stance can be summarized by one sentence: 'We do not accept your hard opinion of yourself!'

The declaration
The following actions were planned: two declarations, one at home in the presence of his siblings and the second at the nursery using a 'sit-in', involving the kids, the nursery teacher and the team.[1] The declarations in both places will be the same and will include clear and categorical objection to any form of Thomas's aggression against himself or others. The parents will also stress their commitment to love and protect him, to refrain from insulting or shouting at him. An apology for all the hurts they may have caused him in the past was included and they underlined their determination that at their home there will be no more shouting and beating. Furthermore, even hugging and kissing will from now on be done only with explicit and mutual permission.

The parents were once more encouraged to bring the situation to the attention of their few friends and work colleagues and to try to get them involved in this intensive process. They were also asked to encourage the nursery team to contact the therapy team and to leave them a copy of the *Guidebook for Parents*. On the following day, the nursery principal contacts the therapy team, and receives coaching on the working principles of the treatment and the manner in which the sit-in is supposed to be carried out. The nursery principal promises her full support and co-operation.

---

1   For a definition of 'declaration' and 'sit-in' see Chapter 10.

THE THIRD SESSION: PARENTAL PRESENCE

The parents report that the two declarations were successful. At the nursery, the declaration was read by the parents and then followed with similar words by each and every nursery team member.

The ensuing discussion focuses on identifying the parents' disengagement process. The parents report that the nursery teacher told them that Thomas's frequent crises have decreased to about one a day and this is dealt with through the 'time-in' method.[2] The parents also report that they had an excellent week and there was no need to have time-in sessions.

Plans to increase the parents' presence and shift them into the family centre were agreed on. The father who works until the late evening will start to make daily calls from work. The aim of such calls is to say 'Hello, I am thinking of you and I am here! I am at work, but I am thinking of you.' In addition to such calls, the father will spend one hour with Thomas, not necessarily at home, on a designated day each week. The father was asked to come up with an idea for fun activity he can undertake with Thomas without feeling childish or ridiculous or fearing that Thomas will reject the idea. At the planning stage, the team keeps emphasizing that in order to increase the parental presence, it is not necessary to make dramatic gestures and that small and sometimes trivial actions can bring about considerable changes.

THE FOURTH SESSION: THE INITIAL CHANGE

The parents arrive at the meeting excited and sound very encouraged by events. The father tells about the experience of the first trip with Thomas in his entire life. The success of the trip generated excited feelings of competence and a strong feeling of fondness towards his son – a feeling, he claims, he had never experienced in his entire relationship with Thomas. He says that he feels like an analphabetic who is being taught to read and write and who experiences the delight of reading the first word. He proceeds to tell that the daily chats from work are gradually becoming easier and that he understands why they are so important. Although uneasy about those calls, this interaction has begun to bear fruit – it seems that both Thomas and the other

---

2   When Thomas acted out, the teacher would take him to another room, and stay with him quietly until he calmed down. At that point, she would return with him to the group. See Chapter 10, p.181.

kids are pleased to speak to him. Even the occupational therapist has noticed a difference and commented that Thomas has turned from a sad to a happy boy.

The mother says that for the first time since she can remember visiting her friends, such a visit turned out to be non-problematic. They went to visit friends and Thomas played without any need for intervention or for protecting the other children. Only when it came time to go away, Thomas refused to go with them and his mother reprimanded him severely while squeezing his hand. When Thomas complained about it, she responded by saying: 'You make me treat you as if you were a sack of potatoes.' To her amazement, Thomas apologized. At this point, the team points out that a better choice of words when she is angry will serve their purpose better and that she is advised to refrain from insulting him or saying anything that damages his self-image. In addition, she is asked categorically to avoid any aggressive physical contact. At the end of the meeting the team emphasizes and reiterates that the fine tuning of the interactions is a never-ending task.

At the same time it is agreed to concentrate on and enjoy the week that has passed. Several recommendations are put forward based on the understanding that lies behind the principle of the model including the idea that physical tenderness is allowed only by permission. It should be valid and exercised at any time, place and with any of the people Thomas interacts with. The point about the need for mutual consent before physical contact and expressions of care are given is stressed. It is agreed that members of the family who are usually very loving, like the grandparents, should also ask permission before hugging and kissing him.

At the end of the meeting the parents plan a special ceremony to be celebrated together with their relatives at their traditional Sunday meal.

THE LAST SESSION: ENTERTAINING HOPE

The parents arrive relaxed but express their concern about losing the support of the therapy team. There are no incidents involving any excessive behaviour of Thomas to report. The father brings Thomas to the nursery without any incidents and there are many 'tantrum-free' mornings. On other mornings, the parents manage to intercept the signs of trouble and calm Thomas down. At the Sunday meal, the family gathered and the planned ceremony took place. The grandfather added a special blessing for Thomas. This was followed in turn by all the participants who congratulated Thomas and his family on his new way.

The parents report that the self-destructive exclamations have stopped altogether and that Thomas's habit of banging his head against the wall has also stopped. At home there has been no need for any time-in sessions. In parallel to the explanations given to their relatives and friends, Thomas started to ask permission to hug and kiss them. The parents have also begun to ask permission before hugging and kissing him and saw to it that the grandparents did likewise. The great importance of the categorical stance concerning personal boundaries, and the non-escalating dialogue that the parents fostered at home, appear to be influencing Thomas's brother. During a fight between them, he stops himself from overreacting and says: 'No beating at our home!'

According to the nursery teacher, there is also improvement there. In spite of some occasions where Thomas had to be told off, no serious incidents have taken place and in some cases, in order to calm Thomas down and prevent escalation, a time-in session was held. The self-destructive exclamations have dropped considerably and Thomas does not disturb the other kids nearly as often as he used to. The nursery team also pointed out that in general Thomas gets along much better with his peers.

Rewriting past experience

The father is particularly excited about his new involvement at home and about his ability to set the tone and offer options without 'threatening' his children. In the morning when he is responsible for bringing Thomas to the nursery, Thomas presents himself proudly to him, fully dressed and exclaiming 'I am ready.' In the last week, as is customary in the nursery, the father stayed to play with Thomas and the kids gathered around to cheer Thomas to victory. The father keeps repeating that he never imagined it to be so easy. He tells the team that he wants to organize a family trip, something that the family did not dare do in the past, in order to 'build a common past and family experiences that we do not have'.

To conclude the therapy, the parents are given a letter that is read by the therapist. The letter examines the treatment's starting point and the aims that were set up. The principles of Non-Violent Resistance are reviewed, along with escalation points and the events that fed them. Emphasis is put on the difficulties that were additional to the core problem, such as the social isolation of the family, the distance from the father's place of work to where the 'action' is, and the tendency of the parents to disengage from the children. The team also reviews the recommendations adopted by the parents and their course of action, as well as their achievements.

The letter emphasizes the clear improvement in the stance and the manner in which the parents conduct their interactions with Thomas. It states that the parents adhered to the instructions, adopted the principles of Non-Violent Resistance and carried out all the recommendations made during the therapy period. This was with the understanding that the efforts should be made even if no immediate change in Thomas's behaviour occurs. The letter expresses appreciation of the effort made in facilitating the move of the 'irrelevant' father from the physical and emotional periphery into Thomas's and the family's central life.

The team concludes with a recommendation for the parents to enjoy and relish in their achievements, to allow new adults to come into their children's lives, and to ensure that the social web surrounding them becomes denser, so that they will be able to gain support and confidence from it. Furthermore, the parents are advised to consider their well-being both individually and as a couple. The two leave the meeting satisfied and encouraged while at the same time apprehensive about facing the future without the therapy that accompanied them thus far.

THE FOLLOW-UP: KEEP GOING

The meeting takes place a month later and the couple display mixed emotions. In spite of the fact that the last month has passed without any major incidents, they point out that Thomas is showing some signs of regression and that they sorely miss the support of the therapy team. Thomas avoids the harsh self-destructive declarations and actions of the past, and the escalating incidents are less frequent. However, in the last week it appears that Thomas is in a bad mood, that his mood swings from one extreme to another and that he complains a lot. The mother adds that by and large the situation has reverted back to the old pattern – she is the one who is in charge of disciplining the kids.

On healing and wanting more

It appears that the Schmidt couple express feelings that are so common after the initial change has taken place. Four weeks after the end of the therapy, the absence of the self-destructive exclamations and acts, tantrum-full mornings and days appears quite natural. Instead of head-banging and suicidal sentiments, Thomas's complaints, mood swings and verbal expressions of anger are now the top of the agenda – this is the new unbearable state of affairs.

The team engages the concerned parents in a reframing exercise to enable them to identify in the current situation the change that took place and the promise of further healing that it carries with it. Thomas gives up his self-destructive and suicidal speech and tantrums in favour of verbal complaints and anger. He uses words to express his discomfort, his dissatisfaction and his anger. In doing this he enables his parents for the first time to enter into a dialogue with him. However, it is a challenging dialogue that requires the parents' commitment to be present, to be physically and emotionally connected to and in tune with their child. The team reminds the parents that from the start the idea that Thomas would probably remain a challenging child was repeatedly emphasized. They have to adhere to the process of change set by the therapy and remember that the main change is the one they make in their reactions. They have to stay calm without losing their nerve whenever Thomas loses his. This is the only way they can bring him to a point where they can calm him down and placate him. They were asked to reflect on how much easier it is to mollify a child who complains than one who shouts 'I deserve to die.'

The mother responds by saying that she does not understand where all the anger and complaints come from. The father adds that even his brother, Eddie, is very negative and behaves as if everyone is ganging up on him: 'If the life-guard blows his whistle, he leaves the pool, being convinced that the whistle was meant for him.' He adds: 'My wife angrily refuses to accept help and the kids react similarly.'

The team exploits the opportunity to discuss why the family members appear to have a constant expectation that something bad is about to happen. They are asked to examine what may be present in their behaviour, both verbally and non-verbally, that gives their kids the feeling of lack of trust and of an impending disaster.

Once more, the team recommends continuing the process of self-exploration and the insistence on recharging themselves as individuals and as a couple, to help with the difficult and tiring parental challenge that lies ahead of them. The team encourages the mother to allow the father more room to manoeuvre with Thomas and to step aside to facilitate this. It is agreed that this is not easy to do, and that it requires her to accept and accommodate the father's slower pace in doing things and to refrain from stepping in and doing it for him. The team emphasizes the need for her to continue to fine tune this new attitude.

In concluding, it was re-emphasized that everything the parents will do in the future must not be examined and evaluated in terms of immediate benefit or result.

CHAPTER SIX

A Barricaded Teenager

Mr and Ms Hernandez are both academics in their early forties and have a son called Robert who is 14 and a half, and two daughters, Diana, who is 11 and Yvonne, who is eight. The father emigrated from Spain and the mother from Sweden. After their marriage they settled in Germany. The mother works for a high-tech company and the father is a civil servant. Both tend to come back fairly late from work and in their absence a care-taker looks after the children.

The referral for therapy was done by the mother through the recommendation of a counsellor from Robert's high school, which he has been attending for three months. The list of Robert's problems that Ms Hernandez provided included barricading himself in his room, turning day into night, refusing to attend school, do any home work or take any responsibility for household chores, consuming alcohol and befriending 'negative' people, aggressive speech and verbal and physical abuse towards his sister and his mother.

THE INTAKE SESSION: ON DISENGAGING

At the point at which the meeting takes place, Robert is suffering from the 'kissing disease' (infectious mononucleosis)[1] and has been at home for ten days. None of his classmates nor the teacher have

---

1   Infectious mononucleosis is an illness caused by a viral infection, most often the Epstein-Barr virus, and has been nicknamed the 'kissing disease' because the virus can be transmitted in saliva during kissing. However, sneezes and coughs can also transmit the virus occasionally. Once a person is infected, the virus remains alive in the body for the rest of his or her life. It often causes only a mild illness, like a cold, or no illness at all. The Epstein-Barr virus permanently infects more than 90 per cent of the world's population, but it causes mononucleosis only in a small minority of them. In developed nations, mononucleosis often develops between the ages of 15 and 25.

made contact or enquired after him. Both parents, but especially the mother, are disturbed by this. According to them, Robert was always an introverted child who had little contact with other children. This tendency increased in the last two years and other problems that were minor in his childhood became more evident. The mother says that 'It was always a struggle to "get into" his mind.' Psychological tests carried out in the past showed him as being a gifted and precocious child with considerable musical talent. He was close to releasing a music CD but his interest evaporated without any apparent reason from one day to the next and nothing came of it. Similarly, many things in which he showed interest and was excited about were suddenly neglected when the activity reached a turning point. He often complains about noise and it appears that the noise and the many children at school cause him distress. He shows considerable sensitivity to smell and checks his food carefully before eating anything and tends to wash several times a day. In addition, he displays some 'tick' such as blinking and nail-biting. The parents recount that at the end of the previous academic year, before going to high school, they helped him with his home work and 'thereby saved his end-of-the-year report', because otherwise he would not have made it to the high school he currently attends.

The process of disengaging from his friends and being absent from school progressed slowly at first. On those occasions when he actually goes to school, he usually arrives late because he finds it extremely difficult to wake up in the morning. At school he does not lift a finger: 'Does not open a book and does not hand in any work.' He frequently declares his hate towards the school and repeatedly says: 'If I could afford it, I'd hire a suicide bomber to blow up the school.'

The parents have supplied Robert with an environment that is highly conducive to him barricading himself and disengaging from the family. His room is equipped with every possible electrical gadget: telephone, computer, electrical keyboard, synthesizer, TV set, amongst others. Most of his time is spent in front of the computer, surfing the web and chatting till the small hours of the night and then sleeping when day time comes. The father leaves home in the early hours of the morning so that the responsibility for getting the children up and to school falls on the mother's shoulders. Getting up and ready for school has become a major battlefield between Robert and his mother, one in which the mother has little chance of winning. On occasions, Robert's mother reverts to hitting him and on one occasion she spilled water over him to wake him up. Another time, she tore his shirt when attempting to get him out of bed. Two weeks before the referral, she tried to wake him up and had to beg, cajole and threaten him through the locked door but to no avail. Eventually she lost control of herself and broke the door down.

Both parents claim that it is difficult to take measures against Robert's excessive use of the internet as it is after all an important channel of communication with the external world for him. It has helped him, in contrast to his reclusive trend, to start a relationship with a few 'nice' girls, and they are loath to restrict him and thereby add to his reclusiveness. For a short while, after the phone bills reached an unprecedented peak, the parents disconnected the phone but could not maintain this for long and re-established the connection. In the summer, they forced him to come abroad with them but he did not agree to do anything with them, slept all day and was surfing the web at night. In a school essay about his holidays, Robert wrote that he preferred not to have contact with kids of his age out of choice.

At home, Robert talks to no one and unless he is confronting someone, keeps silent. The family is so used to his silence, that when he actually speaks to them they do not know what and how to answer: 'We have forgotten how to interact with him.'

The mother sobs when she tells how much Robert loathes her. He finds her voice repulsive and even when she greets him he complains of her shouting at him. When she stands next to him he tells her to 'Go away, you smell.' The mother claims that most of the time she does not respond since it is acceptable that he expresses his opinion and dissatisfaction. She does not mind his aggressive behaviour since she prefers any sort of communication, even negative communication, to his reclusiveness. The family dines together once a week but even this is too much for Robert who refuses to participate and lets the rest of them sit and wait for him to no avail. He plays no role in taking care of the household chores and his attitude is summed up by the parents: 'He doesn't give a damn.'

Mr Hernandez has an extended family and keeps in close contact with them, but Robert refuses to join any of the family reunions. In

Ms Hernandez's view, the family has nothing to contribute to solving Robert's problem.

The parents are impressed by Robert's school. In spite of the fact that his teacher does not know him and the class has not yet gelled together, the school counsellor became aware of his problems. In fact, if it was not for her, they would not have noticed anything amiss. Their distance from Robert and resulting ignorance and lack of ability to notice and identify the problem, makes them feel helpless. It was his art teacher who identified a crisis when looking at one of his drawings and subsequently notified the counsellor. In a conversation with Robert, he told the counsellor that he apparently got a girl from the same school pregnant. She then referred them to a walk-in clinic, where adolescents can seek medical or psychological help in times of need. Robert categorically refused to notify his parents and claimed in a letter to the counsellor that he wanted to bear the responsibility for the case and did not regard the parents as the 'appropriate' address for help. The counsellor delayed notifying the parents using the excuse of protecting the girl's privacy. In the following days, the parents treated Robert with the utmost care and showed no sign of being aware of anything. Robert demonstratively placed the referral note to the adolescence clinic on his table, but his father, who noticed it, was afraid of taking the opportunity to talk about the incident and ended up saying nothing. The pregnancy turned out to be a false alarm.

Following the advice given to them by the counsellor, the parents conduct a search in Robert's room where they find smoking utensils and a considerable amount of alcohol. In the ensuing unavoidable confrontation, the parents confiscate his room key, his TV and his access to the internet. In response, Robert steals a large sum of money and runs away. The parents contact every person who knows Robert and after 'turning the world inside out' they locate him and Mr Hernandez goes to fetch him back.

A short time after his return, as a result of the shock of him running away, the parents lose the courage to proceed with implementing the advice given to them and provide him once more with everything he had before, except the TV set and the key to his room. He signs an agreement with them promising to abstain from alcohol and smoking. At the same time he demands money for the expenses he had when they 'forced' him to escape from home. At this point the school counsellor refers the Hernandez parents to the Non-Violent Resistance therapy team.

With regard to their daughter Diana, the parents say that she is a bit immature and dependent; that she is sometimes noisy without taking notice of other people and that she is capable of harassing Robert in sophisticated ways. She voluntarily recounts events to the parents whenever Robert refuses to tell them anything. Robert beats her up severely and she keeps repeating that he will 'kill her one day'. Recently, after Robert beat her, Mr Hernandez claims that he restrained Robert physically. He then corrects himself and admits to beating Robert and says that since then Robert has stopped beating his sister. However, the verbal abuse goes on, with Robert calling her names and mocking her, especially in the father's absence.

In summary, the understandings reached at the intake session are as follows.

The team acknowledges the deep concern of the parents about Robert's well-being, in particular that of the mother. It was agreed that Robert's behaviour may indicate deep psychological problems and that it may be expedient to encourage him to seek help in the future. Nevertheless, from the overall state of affairs it is clear that the top priority for the parents is to act immediately and increase their involvement in Robert's life.

It was agreed that the parents play a definite role in the escalation of certain confrontations.

Some light is shed over the manner in which adolescents think and reason. This is meant to explain the resistance of Robert to any 'invasion' of his inner world or as the mother puts it: 'He does not like it when someone tries to penetrate his mind.'

It is decided for the time being to ignore Robert's performance at school and to concentrate instead on communication with his parents; the interactions that lead to escalation and to Robert's barricading himself; finding ways to break his self-imposed isolation; and the principle that every reaction should be well thought out and carried out in a quiet, persistent and assertive manner. In addition, any interactions and any measures taken should under no circumstances be influenced or dictated by Robert's reaction or willingness to co-operate.

The parents are requested to read the *Guidebook for Parents* and to prepare for the next meeting:

- a list of possible openings in Robert's barricade
- a list of potential support people
- ideas for the declaration.

THE FIRST SESSION: BREAKING THE BARRICADE

The parents arrive well prepared and convinced that the *Guidebook for Parents* was written especially for Robert. Robert is still ill and a tense silence dominates the house. The parents point to several things that can be used to break down his barricade: his illness and his need to be looked after, his love of music, his apparent desire to succeed, his response to a physical challenge, his plan for his room's renovations and his fondness for attending the church.

A brainstorming session produces the following ideas:

Robert's illness

A ready-made opening is his illness which gives them the chance of getting him out of his room and gaining entry to his room. During his illness, many of the confrontations revolving around getting up in the morning and doing home work are irrelevant and can be put aside. This is therefore a perfect opportunity to make all the gestures of conciliation, care and attention, such as accompanying Robert to the feared blood test that he has to take. It is also an opportunity to establish a link between the outside world and Robert at home in his fort – his room. It is necessary to allow other adults to enter his life, to come and 'disturb' him by knocking on his door and being able to express interest and care. It is imperative to get his teacher and classmates to make contact, enquire after him and come and visit him.

The TV set is not to be re-installed in his room, in spite of his pleas, in order to make the environment external to his room more tempting. Nice food, beautiful music, get-togethers – sitting and having relaxed conversations, drinking hot chocolate, filling the place with the smell of baking and cooking – will all contribute towards creating an appealing atmosphere. In addition, a decision to have a common light meal in the evening is made. The problem of not attending school is put aside for the time being.

Music

The parents should take a real interest in the music of his liking and ask to listen to it. In addition, they can enable him to show off his expertise and ability by asking him to search for the music that they liked when they were young.

Room renovation

The original idea was to turn the basement into 'Robert's castle'. However, having seen how he barricades and isolates himself it has become clear that they must not move him away from the house centre. They decide to use the excuse of limited finances as the reason for the change and instead suggest renovating his current room. This will enable them to install a door without a key-lock in his room. During the renovations Robert will have to share his sister's room.

Physical challenge

In the summer holidays abroad, the parents noticed that any trip that required physical exertion was welcomed by Robert. The father will therefore try and engage Robert in gardening activities.

Family gatherings might also be a good idea. The parents must accept the idea that they are not capable of addressing Robert and his problems alone, and that the external world can offer much needed help and support for the required change. The father's family can play an important role in this and should be brought in to help in spite of the mother's strong opinion. It is decided to encourage Robert to be physically active by assigning him clear duties in the planned family get-together, such as sharing the responsibility for the shopping and preparations.

A friendship that Robert had with the daughter of his parents' friends was broken when he insulted her. A decision was taken to renew the contact by involving the friends and organizing a reconciliation between Robert and the girl.

Church visits

Robert used to like going to the church with his family to attend Sunday prayers. These visits were stopped due to the father's time constraints and were not renewed in spite of Robert's request. It was therefore decided to renew this tradition and the festive Sunday meal that accompanied it.

THE SECOND SESSION: THE DREAM AND THE DECLARATION

The session begins with Mr Hernandez recounting Robert's dream. The family and Robert are on a trip when he enters a car that suddenly starts to roll. He does not know what to do and his parents look on without getting involved. The obvious interpretation of this dream is that, as parents, they must use the brakes where he cannot as they cannot allow him to roll downhill uncontrollably and to go far too fast. The dream poses an excellent opportunity to legitimize parental intervention – to allow the parents to facilitate 'solid driving at the right speed'. As the rationale for parental intervention it is possible to say to Robert: 'Your dream reinforces the need for us to be more involved in your life.'

The dream serves as a natural link to the preparation of the declaration that will address three issues: barricading himself in the room, verbal and physical violence, and alcohol and drug abuse.

Earlier signs of closeness between Robert and his father influence the decision to let the father read the declaration to Robert. An opening line is suggested: 'We have considered the situation, have deliberated long and hard and have reached the conclusion that a change in our lives is necessary. The state of affairs at home has reached an unbearable level for all of us. Harsh exchanges among us, you barricading yourself in your room, your abuse of your mother and sister, the long hours spent before the TV and surfing the internet.'

At the same time, the demand that he avoid barricading himself in his room can be related to his illness and his need for help and can be expressed as: 'We cannot allow you to stay with a locked door given your illness.' The objection to the use of alcohol and drugs as well as the objection to his verbal and physical abuse of his mother and sister should be stated in a clear and unequivocal manner. The parents are asked to be specific: 'We cannot allow you to beat Diana or call her names!'

The parents are also instructed to refer to the content of the letter Robert wrote his school counsellor where he described his parents as selfish, quick to get angry and as taking too much responsibility for themselves. He has to be told: 'Parallel to our attempts to control your activities, we promise to try and limit the extent of our interference in your life, but we cannot allow you to jeopardize your health and your life.'

The declaration should end with the statement: 'We have no desire to subdue you but to follow the feelings we feel towards you and fulfil our duty to look after your well-being. We appreciate your desire for independence and the effort you are making to achieve this; nevertheless we have the privilege and duty to try to look after you as well as we can.'

A discussion, revolving around the theme of how to show care and respect when interacting with an adolescent, followed. Instead of asking 'I would like to know how you feel' or 'What are you feeling?', it may be more constructive to say 'I see that you are not feeling well' or 'I sense you are not at your best, is there any way I can help?' The natural tendency of the adolescent is to reject any such attempts but the different tone and style would make it much harder to do so.

After an examination of the openings in Robert's fortifications and the planning of the declaration, the same question that arose during the intake session was brought up: how is Robert's exhaustion to be interpreted? At the intake meeting, the possibility of drugs as the cause for his tiredness and lack of energy was rejected out of hand by the parents and these were instead attributed to his 'kissing disease'. The father insists that he does not understand when Robert can use drugs given the level of supervision that they exercise on him. The fact that alcohol and cigarettes were found in his room does not prove that he is using drugs. In the father's view, Robert locks the door because of his need for intimacy and privacy. This pattern has already manifested itself at the intake meeting; the parents almost reach an inevitable conclusion but out of fear of the consequences of such a conclusion, they back off and find an alternative and inappropriate explanation.

To conclude the meeting the parents are requested to pay attention to:

- The acts of aggression that they carry out as well as verbal aggression in the form of endless preaching, endless attempts to convince, constant playing on Robert's guilt feelings, threats and the like. Such acts only serve to amplify the escalation and feed the disengagement from each other, sometimes fulfilling an authentic need but at other times being used as an excuse. These exchanges create a sense of helplessness and incompetence in the parents.

- Examples of how some of their well-intentioned efforts only made the situation worse in the case of doing Robert's home work, taking responsibility for getting him up in the morning to go to school, and the well-cushioned environment in his room that enables and encourages him to disengage from his surroundings and switch from real to virtual relationships.

The parents are also requested to consider the avoidance mechanism in which they operate:

- Their constant fear that Robert will not co-operate with them, as in the case of the pregnancy. (In this incident, Robert in fact appeared to have invited them to intervene by placing the referral right under their noses. Yet in spite of the demonstrative manner of his doing so, his father chose to ignore it.)

- Their tendency to refrain from acting where it is needed for fear that the situation will deteriorate. (Worse still, after imposing sanctions they fail to follow through, as in his last escape from home.)

- To be aware and ready to recognize signs of possible use of drugs.

THE THIRD SESSION: HESITATION

The parents return defeated and desperate. The Easter holiday is fast approaching and the declaration event has not taken place. While they were waiting for the appropriate moment, Robert returned to school and the situation at home deteriorated and the opportunities that appeared in the previous meeting now seem impossible. Ms Hernandez excuses herself by saying that she waited for the optimal moment but it did not arrive. In the meantime Robert is back to his old habits, chatting and surfing the web into the small hours and not getting up in the morning. In light of all of this they think that what they wanted to say in the declaration is too weak! Robert continues to taunt Diana and the mornings are a battlefield. He took back his promise to come with them on a weekend trip and the trip was therefore cancelled. The reconciliation attempt with the friend's daughter was not successful. She refused to meet him because she was still hurt. In general they cannot agree on a declaration format and context.

The declaration

The team clarifies once more the nature of the declaration: the declaration is not an act that is aimed at changing the child but a proclamation of the full responsibility that the parents are assuming on the state of affairs, on looking after the child to prevent the situation from deteriorating, without any expectations of the result. The text is examined once more and suggestions such as an opening that says: 'We will embrace your development and address your needs, but if your independence will turn to reclusiveness, we will do anything in our means to fight it. We will not accept your disengagement. Normal life means to get up in the morning and face the job and responsibilities that go with it. Your job is to go to school and study and your place is in the family with us.'

The mother keeps coming back with doubts and is sure that Robert will respond by saying: 'This declaration proves that you do not understand me.' In a similar fashion, when he mistreats his sister the mother sees no point in saying anything to him since he is likely 'not to give a damn about it'.

The team points out to her that it is of importance to Robert what other people think about him and advises acting on it. It is possible to say to him: 'We feel alone in this case and therefore we are going to seek external help.' The team suggests mentioning in the declaration the referral to therapy: 'The situation among us is difficult to the point of being unbearable and turning to external advice has made several issues clearer.' Public opinion can be exploited as a tool. The external world needs to be brought into the home and like a Greek choir repeat the parents' utterances: 'Mistreating your siblings is unacceptable to us.' It is time to act and not be held back by Robert's lack of response.

The mother is still perplexed about the declaration, the sit-ins and the enlisting of external people. She keeps coming back to a feeling of helplessness and keeps falling back to a sense of incompetence. It is unclear to her what she can do with the given tools. In spite of the guidelines, and the detailed instructions face to face and over the phone, she still claims to be helpless and lacking tools to deal with the situation.

The summary of the meeting asks the parents to pay attention to:

- avoiding being dragged into escalating situations, reducing endless talk, enlisting public opinion, making the declaration and sit-ins
- moving from hesitation to action: there is no need to wait for an ideal time
- planning the reaction to possible drug abuse.

In summarizing, the team emphasizes that the actions are effective only as long as they state a clear position that they repeat themselves consistently and quietly. To the question 'And what then?' there is but one answer: 'I will persevere because that is all I have.' The parents are once more asked and encouraged to cast their doubts aside and get on with it.

THE FOURTH SESSION: TIME TO ACT

The Hernandez family experiences a difficult week. The denial of the previous meeting is replaced with the disappointment that Robert has deceived them all the while. One night, the parents let Robert believe that they are asleep and when he left the house after neutralizing the alarm, the mother followed him to the park and found him lying there helpless having passed out. Upon searching his room, they find hashish. On the same night the parents turned to the police and suggested creating a 'warning' file for him. The parents also turned to an anti-drug association that provides help and advice regarding drug abuse and how to deal with it. Robert agreed to have periodical checks but denied having smoked dope. On the following evening the declaration was carried out with all of his friends in attendance. Mr Hernandez addresses Robert's friends: 'I have no desire to threaten you but the fact that you used drugs incriminates you.' At the same time he assures them that he has no intention of turning to their parents or the police. When he requested information about the source of the drugs, he was met with silence from all of them.

The parents have different recollections of the event. The father recalls that when talking to his friends, Robert sat and listened patiently.

The mother on the other hand remembers him as being extremely embarrassed and uncomfortable. This characterizes the father's tendency to identify co-operation while the mother interprets everything as a failure to influence what she perceives as her son's 'personality disorder'.

Recurring doubts

Mr Hernandez wants to enlist the parents of the other children in order to have more involved and observant participants. But once more, doubt strikes; he agonizes over whether to involve the other parents, fearing that their harsh reaction may harm their children. In any case, Easter is approaching and he does not wish to encumber the family at this point with such a message and prefers to act after the holidays. The mother seconds him and claims that it will be more beneficial to concentrate on the child since he needs treatment. She concludes by saying that 'We have a disturbed child.' While claiming that she does not wish to change him, she sees his problem and is sure that without therapy 'nothing will change'. If he was happy, she would have no problem with him barricading himself in his room, adding 'For two years I find myself resisting and nothing happens. Since finding the drug, he excludes us from his life even more than before and we are treated like lepers.' In general, she perceives a sit-in session as irrelevant and ineffective.

The team sees it quite differently. The sit-ins re-introduce the parents' involvement that is so fragile and under threat in this case. The drug and the reclusiveness problems are tied together. They acknowledge that he may indeed have psychological problems. However, it is not possible to force Robert to undergo therapy. On the other hand, it *is* possible to exploit the tools at hand and modify the parents' behaviour and attitude. It is clear that what can be modified, and made stable and constant, is their own behaviour – becoming quieter, more persistent, and avoiding being dragged into unnecessary confrontations. At this point, the mother states that as far as she is concerned the penny has finally dropped.

The team keeps emphasizing that this is the right time to act and to do so in a well-planned manner with reachable and carefully placed goals. The father considers delaying until after Easter but the team emphasizes the need to act immediately. Moreover, the team recommends getting in touch with all of Robert's friends. This exercise is meant to find as many people as possible who are willing to co-operate and look after Robert.

The meeting ends with the following agreement:

- The parents will arrange a sit-in in Robert's room and repeat the ideas put forward in the declaration.

- The father will enlist one of Robert's friends to talk to him.

THE LAST SESSION: ONE STEP SHORT

The parents arrive with an impressive list of implementations and successes. They announce that an appropriate occasion was found immediately following the last session for a sit-in in Robert's room. They used this opportunity to re-issue the declaration with emphasis on the 'barricading' phenomenon that had become worse since the discovery of drug abuse. To their surprise and contrary to their worst fears that had prevented them from acting so far, apart from some protest when they entered the room, the incident passed without any significant drama. When the second version of the declaration was read through, the parents declared that they would sit and wait until Robert made a constructive suggestion for addressing the problem and left it at that. After a prolonged silence, he told his parents that he is not willing to accept their intervention in his life, but is willing to take part in the family life. The agreement reached on this occasion has the following surprising effects:

- Robert asks permission to leave the house, something he has not done for years.

- He expresses a desire to participate in family events.

- The father asked his brother to talk to Robert, to invite him to celebrate Easter together with the family. Robert met him and in a long conversation agreed to help organize a big barbecue for the large family. He seemed delighted with the praise he got. Ms Hernandez is astounded by the way he reacted; she never imagined things turning out that way.

- Since his return, the parents give him chores at home and in the garden and Robert does them.

- To cap it all, Robert has agreed to join them for a visit to his parents' friends that he has never met before.

The parents feel that the timing of the sit-in was right and that the action was fruitful. They found a crack in their son's fortifications. The two appear intoxicated when they describe how the day before Robert helped with household chores in the garden, then stayed with them and then fell asleep on the sofa. Robert has come out from the barricades, is active and allows his parents to participate in his life. The intervention has achieved its goal for the time being. Nevertheless, the parents are not satisfied with this and outline a vigorous plan to return Robert to an intensive school regime. The team's insistence, heard throughout this intervention, that Robert's performance at school is not the central issue of the relationship is rejected vehemently by Ms Hernandez. Throughout the intervention period, Mr Hernandez keeps saying that Robert 'needs treatment for his personality disorder'.

It is apparent that the parents act when necessary and take the right action but often fail to act all the way. They know a lot about their son, but they always remain one step, one clue short of putting the jigsaw together. It is as if they lack the strength or the will to take the final step where necessary. They go to the police and also to the anti-drug association but alone, without Robert. Robert agrees to have drug tests but these are conducted at home. They hesitate to make contact with the parents of his drug abuse accomplices with the excuse that they do not want to spoil their holidays. They are afraid of talking to other parents from fear of their reaction.

The parents' fear of losing control over their child's inner world and the mother's insistence that Robert has a personality disorder is discussed again. The team tries to reframe the parents' attitude on such issues by repeatedly stating that it is legitimate to let an adolescent make mistakes and also fail – but at the same time it is also legitimate to want to keep an eye on him and to safeguard his well-being. However, this must be done at the right level and dosage; monitoring to minute detail and trying to micro-manage suffocates the adolescent as well as the parents. Exercising too detailed and strict observation and control runs the risk of not seeing the wood for the trees. Furthermore, it prevents the parents from seeing the adolescent as a person in his own right and from interacting with him in a healthy manner. It is necessary to relinquish some of that strict control in favour of a respectful level of contact that allows the parents to look after the well-being of Robert without restricting his need for independence. Understanding this and relinquishing their desire for optimal control is a key step for the parents. The initial progress made by the parents is the basis from which the struggle with the problems that lie ahead will be conducted.

The summary brings up the following points:

- Agreement of the progress and achievements from the intervention.
- Robert and his parents have renewed communication.
- It is imperative to allow Robert to maintain his inner world to himself.

At the same time the parents must strive to maintain their parental presence in a consistent and persistent manner and be unapologetic when it concerns his safety and well-being, as in the excessive internet use and drug abuse. Where escalation occurs, like running away, the parents can revert to the tools described in the *Guidebook for Parents*.

THE FOLLOW-UP: WHEN THE THERAPIST IS GONE

On the night of the fourth meeting, after the parents go to bed, they hear Robert leaving the house and follow him to discover him in the park lying on one of the benches, pale, incoherent and in possession of drugs. The parents repeat the ritual of turning to the anti-drug association and Robert reacts as in the previous occasion by running, and this time staying away for three days. The parents make a list of everyone who knows Robert and contact everyone. The father locates him in the north and goes there, even though he knows Robert is already on the way back but not home. His intention is to talk to the girl who hosted him and with her parents. Following the therapy approach, he makes a point of establishing contact, even though Robert is no longer there, thereby making a statement of being present.

In the meantime Ms Hernandez discovers, through a list of Robert's internet chats that he is in frequent contact with a mature person, conducting long chats often late at night. Their correspondence reveals instructions of how to grow 'grass' in the garden. When the father returns they contact this person and demand to see him.

The meeting takes place on the following day. A man in his thirties appears with his female partner and claims that Robert showed up at their flat the day before and asked for a place to stay. Seeing that he was in a bad state, they had let him stay. The man insists that throughout the correspondence, he had not realized that he was corresponding with a minor. The couple recommends not forcing Robert to go back home and promise to bring him to school the following day. To the astonishment of the team, just when the parents are at a point where they can establish and confirm their parental presence, they back off and allow an unknown and somewhat suspicious couple to deal with their child. All of this is somehow justified because 'Robert is in a terribly agitated state and may react harshly'.

Although his identity should have been clear by now, it requires a brain-storming session to bring the parents to the conclusion that this man and the 'grass expert' are one and the same. The parents, once again, have not read the map because they cannot face the facts. The team insists that they must act formally yet the parents' pattern of hesitation strikes again and they decide that instead of contacting the police, they will commission a lawyer to write to him and insist on breaking any ties with Robert given the fact that he is still a minor.

In the following month, the parents report a fundamental change taking place in Robert. He co-operates on all fronts and it appears that smoking grass was the cause of him barricading himself and his constant exhaustion. Waking up and going to school is no longer a problem and Robert participates in family life and does household chores. The father finds out who the drug supplier is and the school plans to take steps to remove Robert from his mates. The original goals have been achieved according to Ms Hernandez.

At the end of this meeting several things become clear. Everything done so far was the preparation for mending the relationship with Robert. The parents are requested to stay vigilant and involved in Robert's everyday life without demanding control or 'penetration' into his mind. Gestures of love and reconciliation must be made regardless of his behaviour. The parents will make an effort to aid Robert in creating new connections at school by talking to his teachers, and will also endeavour to maintain a network of friends and support for them and for Robert. His parents should make a continuous effort to relinquish their pattern of hesitation and instead act without backing off at the last step.

SUMMARY

This case presents a number of typical aspects of the work with adolescents and the pitfalls that are often encountered. It is important to define a new set of goals by creating and modifying, within the short therapy span, the priorities and goals of the parents. In this case, for example, it is clearly highly difficult to convince a family who holds academic achievement as sacred, to put such aspirations aside within the first meeting. Another issue to be resolved is the parents' acting on two contradictory planes. On the one hand, they control and micromanage. On the other hand, at the most critical times, they lose their courage to act to exercise their control. Similarly, the constant search for the optimal timing is a trap. The reluctance of Robert's parents to make the declaration and use the sit-in tool until an optimal point is found, paralyses them.

A reluctance to change which conserves patterns of interaction is a classical example of the see-saw action where parental hesitation and lack of action enforce the old habits of Robert and at the same time weaken the parents' ability to look after him. Whenever the hesitation manifests itself, Robert becomes stronger and more confrontational than before. The parents' hesitation allows him to get his way; as a result, his resolve to maintain those patterns of interaction grows and with them his addiction to them.

CHAPTER SEVEN

A Teen at Risk

Mary and her family are a good example of the promise our working model offers for families. Our aim is to create suitable conditions for the empowerment of the parent and the welfare of the child. As in most cases, the vulnerable and helpless mother applies for the intervention with a firm conviction of having an impossible child to manage. All of the blame lies upon the shoulders of the teenage Mary who is perceived as aggressive, manipulative and risk-taking. By the end of the intervention, the mother sees her differently.

We will see how the process of the mother abandoning helplessness becomes a process of unburdening the child as well. This case enables us to track easily how the emphasis on an outright moral stand, as dictated by the model, guides all parental statements – be they verbal or demonstrative. And while the reframing of speech and action presented by the therapist helps to remodel the picture presented at the beginning of the intervention, a new perspective of the situation emerges. In a short time span what was unbearable and threatening becomes a matter for planning and deliberate action.

At 38, Mrs Braun has two children: Mary, aged 14, and Jeffery, aged 11. She divorced six years before and is a financial consultant by profession. Her daughter Mary is the reason for turning to us. Mary's father is 54 years old; he has remarried and has a three-year-old son from his second marriage. He maintains telephone contact with his children and visits them once a week for about an hour. Every two weeks they go to him for the weekend; the visit lasts, according to Mrs Braun, 'exactly 24 hours'.

From the first phone call, Mrs Braun sounds eager to start the intervention. When she finds out that she will have to wait two months until it begins, she protests vigorously, asserting that the situation at home is far too serious to endure such a long delay. She maintains this urgent, anxious tone throughout most of the sessions. To the structured questions posed at the intake, she provides chaotic answers loaded with minor, unnecessary details. Her report is especially difficult to follow as she confuses the order of events. Only in response to the team members' insistent question, does she come forth with extremely important information. We will find out at the first session that she had omitted some vital information during the intake.

THE INTAKE SESSION: ON HIGH AND LOW EXPECTATIONS

Mrs Braun comes to the session alone, even though we had clearly stressed the importance of the father joining the intervention during our telephone conversation. When asked why the father did not come, she pretended that we had never mentioned it. She went on to say that the father does not believe in psychology and that the concepts being discussed are too abstract and may be beyond his understanding. At the same time, she stresses that he would agree to join but only if the times were convenient for him. Throughout the session Mrs Braun emphasizes their cultural differences. She was born and educated in America, whereas he hails from East Germany.

According to Mrs Braun, Mary's troubles pre-dated the divorce. Already in kindergarten she had difficulty relating to children of her own age. In school, Mary shows no interest in her studies and year after year she fails all subjects. At the time of the intake, the principal of her school feels she does not stand a chance in the coming exams. There is only one school left which may be willing to accept her and he maintains 'that will also end in failure'. The future he envisions for Mary is that she will quickly join 'The Kiosk Track' (a slang expression which refers to high school students who do go to school but do not enter the classroom and instead hang out at the nearby kiosk or snack bar).

Although she shows some interest in music, Mary has not kept up any of her music classes. She is not willing to accept any type of authority or discipline. She also refuses to attend her extra tutoring sessions, complaining that her studies are demanding enough and extra hours only harm, and do not help, her. Mary's motto is: 'Next year it will be better.'

At home, she is also uninterested and apathetic. She has a very difficult relationship with her younger brother, fighting with him incessantly, losing control quickly and typically ending the fight with verbal and physical abuse. This includes throwing things at him, slapping him and limiting his movement. Consequently, he regularly barricades himself in his room and refuses to be alone with her, demanding a babysitter in the event that his mother is absent.

Mary spends her free time in front of the computer, sleeping, eating and smoking in her room, in spite of her mother's strenuous objections to her smoking. Although she is overweight, she avoids physical activity, including her gym class. Her weight problem preoccupies Mary and serves as a source of deep distress for her and her mother.

Mrs Braun describes Mary as someone who is often sick. Her paediatrician concurs, adding that many times her symptoms are simply an act. Four months before the intake, Mary complains of intense appendix pain and is rushed to the hospital but further examination yields no other signs. Based on the description of the pain, the doctors decide to operate so as not to take a risk, only to find out that the operation was unnecessary. On another occasion, Mary collapses while running in gym class, and is again rushed to the hospital where she is put on an intravenous infusion. According to Mrs Braun, this was also an act to gain attention – to bring her father to her and to avoid attending school.

Mrs Braun describes a long history of psychological treatments that either failed or were terminated prematurely. Many counsellors came and went and many promises were made but not fulfilled. When Mary was ten and her parents were newly divorced, the family moved to another city and Mary's problems worsened. Upon seeing her once, the psychologist at the public mental health clinic saw no reason to continue treatment, claiming that priority must be given to more serious cases. In junior high school, a rumour was spread that Mary intended to commit suicide. The school refused to allow her to attend, unless she saw a psychologist. She attended only one session and refused to co-operate. Nevertheless, the psychologist determined that she was not suicidal. At 12 she underwent psychological testing, which showed that she did not have learning disabilities, yet she did have emotionally-based attention deficit disorder. However, at this point, Mary totally opposed any form of therapy. The mother joined a support group for divorced mothers, attended two half-year Adlerian[1] courses, and underwent various therapies, the last of which went on for the half year before the beginning of the intervention. The therapist advised her to bring Mary, but Mary came only once and refused to co-operate. Mrs Braun states at this point that in her opinion, Mary is the source of most of her problems.

Mrs Braun describes her relationship with her daughter as very strained – replete with fierce fights and screaming from both about Mary's studies, her provocative appearance and her harsh treatment of her brother. During the last year the tension in their relationship has escalated, although some affection and humour remains intact. Mary comes and goes as she pleases, rejecting her mother's authority outright. At nights, when her mother goes to sleep, she leaves the house without her mother's knowledge and returns at dawn.

In Mrs Braun's words, 'There are good things…when we are in a good period there is a lot of openness. She is very aware of my expectations. Even though I am lowering them all the time they are still high. I've spoken to her about her studies, about university and the army, although it doesn't seem quite realistic to me. In better periods, Mary tries to show me that she can still do it. There is humour and we laugh, it is a bit *fake*, maybe on both sides but mostly from her, but I'm not sure… There is always some type of *manipulation* going on.' About the less good days the mother says, 'I have not found a solution except that the good times are getting increasingly fewer and far between.'

As examples, Mrs Braun describes two typical scenarios that take place in her interactions with Mary. In the first scenario, Mary opposes her mother but is still calm: 'She sits and explains to me why I don't understand – she is very articulate – and then we get into a debate.' In the second scenario, harsh confrontations arouse a sense of fear and hopelessness in Mrs Braun. 'I am terrified and I don't know what to do – to threaten or not. The last time I threatened that I would call

---

1   Alfred Adler (1870–1937) was the founder of the school of individual psychology. Along with Freud, he was among the co-founders of the psychoanalytic movement. Ultimately, he broke away from psychoanalysis to form an independent school of psychotherapy and personality theory. Among other innovations, he espoused the development of democratic family structures as the ideal ethos for raising children.

the police but my threats fall on deaf ears. Mary just goes about her business.' When her mother forbids her to leave, Mary simply gets up and goes. 'Arguments are left open and then they just disappear. We get up in the morning and there is something like remorse, some attempt to appease me. After a fight, Mary will come to my bed to wish me a good morning.' Here, the team encourages the mother that in spite of everything, Mary is still attempting to make peace with her. However, Mrs Braun claims that whereas in the past it might have worked, these days it is very hard for her to accept it.

A recurrent theme in their fights is Mary's claim that both her mother and father do not love her and that her younger brother is more loved. Every argument ends with Mary's relentless protest: 'This is not America. You do not understand the mentality...you are foreign,' which Mrs Braun finds highly insulting.

Mrs Braun is away from home most of the day and her work demands that she travel abroad regularly. A housekeeper is hired to keep house and to take care of the children's needs. Many housekeepers have come and gone, none of them stay for any period of time, due to Mary's incessant screaming and threatening her brother and the housekeeper.

The mother has no family in Germany. Although she has some good friends, they do not know her children. In spite of her claims that they are all on good terms with the father's family, there is no meaningful figure there in Mary's life, except for Mary's father. In fact, Mrs Braun does not believe there is any adult figure that is capable of influencing her. Mary is friendly with two older girls who come from difficult backgrounds. Although Mrs Braun does not know them personally and they do not come to the house, she is still unhappy with their friendship. Naturally, she emphasizes, she does not know the parents of such girls. In fact, Mrs Braun does not know any of Mary's classmates' parents.

Already at the beginning of the intake, it becomes clear that there will be a need to prioritize her thoughts according to their significance and sort out the contradictions. For example, very significant events such as the suicide rumour or the appendectomy are casually mentioned almost at the end of the intake. The casual manner in which she mentions such dramatic events also raises questions. What occupies her and alarms her most is Mary's absence from school and

the looming prospect of her dropping out. The implications of these –
the inability to serve in the US army or attend university – fill her with
fear and anxiety. The mother's preoccupation with schooling seems to
overshadow the real problem.

The team reassures Mrs Braun that first and foremost, her worry
for Mary is justified and that it is indeed time to act. They explain that
understandably she is highly emotional about the report of the events.
Therefore, for clarity's sake, they will attempt to summarize her report
in a few clear and concise points. This will serve to highlight those
elements that fuel her sense of helplessness as well as to determine the
goals of the joint endeavour.

The summary of the points presented to her is as follows:

1. There is a long history of failed psychological treatments.

2. The mother has a right and an obligation to know Mary's
   whereabouts; her forays at night are indeed a cause for
   concern.

3. Mrs Braun's concern about Mary's absence from school is
   legitimate. However, the focus must be shifted to a more
   fundamental concern for Mary's physical and emotional
   heath.

4. All acts that have been deemed as manipulative, if their purpose
   was to draw her parent's attention or to serve as an excuse to
   avoid school, are to be seen as extreme and worrisome acts
   that require both parents' evaluation.

5. Communication with Mary is too wordy – arguments,
   shouting, cursing and unfulfilled threats. Although there are
   some peaceful intervals, they are fewer and farther between
   as the aggressive and forceful confrontations take over. These
   intervals are losing their efficacy and meaning while the lines
   of communication are eroding.

6. Mrs Braun has unrealistic expectations of Mary. Not deliberately nor consciously, Mrs Braun repeatedly communicates
   her disappointment with Mary and with who she is likely
   to be.

7. Mrs Braun is a present-absent parent. Mary is left to her own resources for hours and days, under the care of a housekeeper who can hardly cope with the task at hand.

8. Mrs Braun conveys an ambivalent, at times condescending, attitude to the environment in which she lives, to the father of her children and to his culture, leaving her children feeling insecure and distressed.

9. Mrs Braun leads a dual life. On the one hand, she is anchored in the reality in which she lives, by virtue of her children. On the other hand, she has chosen work that distances her from her surroundings, and takes her literally and figuratively outside of Germany.

10. The father too is an absent-present parent, available to his children only for strictly budgeted, pre-assigned, brief periods of time. The guaranteed way for Mary to get his unconditional attention is to act out by endangering herself.

11. Although Mrs Braun emphasizes how important Mary's father is to her, she undermines him by questioning his intelligence and competence and by refusing to ask him to join the intervention.

12. The family is isolated socially. Aside from the care-givers, they have no social contact with other adults or peers and the mother does not encourage and cultivate contact with other people.

13. The younger brother must be protected from Mary's violence towards him.

As Mrs Braun's report is so confused, there is a need to clarify what must be addressed and in what order. Therefore, from this summary, the team identifies five key points of weakness that are contributing to Mary's vulnerability and extreme behaviour as well as feeding Mrs Braun's helplessness.

1. *Ambivalence:* Mrs Braun's attitude undermines the reality in which her family lives, creating vulnerability and insecurity in her children.

2. *Misguided focus:* concern for Mary's performance at school clouds over Mrs Braun's awareness of the severity of her child's fragile emotional state, as expressed through her violent and dangerous behaviour.

3. *Misinterpretation:* instead of seeing Mary's alarming behaviour as an expression of her vital need for attention and her need for her father's presence, Mrs Braun interprets it as manipulation.

4. *Lack of presence:* Mrs Braun needs to identify and recognize that along with her physical absence at home, she is also emotionally absent. Both forms of absence threaten her children's well-being, as well as her own.

5. *Social isolation:* the family's social isolation weakens Mrs Braun and her children, enabling cycles of escalation and violence to occur unopposed.

Mrs Braun responds to the team's summary with amazement. She remarks that she has never reflected upon her reality with this perspective. At the same time, she agrees with what has been said. The team quickly takes advantage of this, strongly advising that she involve the father in the intervention, instructing her to give him the *Guidebook for Parents* to read and asking her to urge him to come to the next session. The team stresses how important it is to involve others, that abandoning isolation is the primary and essential condition in the struggle to restore Mary's emotional health. Moreover, the struggle for Mary's well-being is essentially the struggle for the entire family's well-being.

The team indicates that the first step in this process is to present the rationale of the intervention to the father and to encourage him to join. Mrs Braun responds to this with the same hesitation and ambivalence towards the father that she originally expressed at the beginning of the intake. 'It is hard for me to believe that he will read the material…it is hard for me to believe that he will understand what is written…I can explain it to him…' At this point she reveals a new and very significant element that she had hitherto concealed. '*He will want his daughter to live with him and that is one of my fears…that he will take her.* I don't believe it will be better for her there.' These last words that seal the meeting, shed light on the essence of the conflict, pointing us to what will be the crux of this particular intervention.

Following up on the fear which Mrs Braun expresses, the team explains to her that she will have to make a choice between stagnation and action. As action always involves risk, she must decide that she is willing to act to heal her daughter, in spite of her fear of Mary moving in with her father. The team encourages her to go through with the intervention and not to allow her fear to thwart her attempts to help her daughter.

At the end of the intake meeting, the goal of intervention is to tackle Mary's primary issues:

- to pursue the source of the recurring complaints of various illnesses
- to battle the violent outbursts against her brother
- to stop her disappearances in the middle of the night
- to build up rapport with Mary's father.

The intake meeting ends with the team handing Mrs Braun the *Guidebook for Parents* as well as recommending that she immediately implement the passive tools mentioned therein, such as the principle of 'not being drawn in' and the 'pause and postpone' principle. The active tools, she is told, will be discussed at the next meeting.

THE FIRST SESSION: ON ANXIETY AND VIOLENCE

Both parents show up at the session. Mr Braun introduces himself and appears to be relaxed. He certainly does not look like a person who was coerced into coming and the team applauds his decision to join. The session opens with the report of the team member who had conducted the telephone support calls to Mrs Braun during the week preceding the session. According to him, the mother reported that there were many difficult outbursts, the source of which was unclear. At the same time, she informed him that by activating the principles of 'not being drawn in' and 'pause and postpone', she had managed to respond with restraint, even succeeding at appeasing Mary after each incident. Here Mrs Braun interrupts his report by interjecting that all of this applies until the weekend. Over the weekend, some very important news came to light which Mary took extremely hard. 'Since yesterday,' the mother says, 'we are in the middle of a real crisis on the issue of moving. Mary expressed feelings that she had never articulated so explicitly before, like suicide threats and extremely harsh language against me and her father, who was present at the time.'

The team, particularly the member who had conducted the support calls, listens with surprise to Mrs Braun's description of the events. At the weekend, Mrs Braun informed Mr Braun of a new job offer that she has decided to accept. The new firm requires her to move her residence to be near her new workplace, which happens to be the city where the father lives. Figuring that the prospect of moving closer to the father will soften the blow of the news, the two of them proceed to inform Mary. This unleashes a litany of severe grievances against her parents coupled with hysterical crying and threats. Mary accuses her mother of being egotistic and sadistic, deriving pleasure from inflicting pain on her. At the same time, Mary reiterates her intention to commit suicide if the plan materializes. The fact that that the move is to her father's city does not comfort or calm her. For his part, her brother locks himself in his room as Mary's response reverberates though the entire house. The parents are overwhelmed by the intensity of this unprecedented reaction which goes on until the small hours of the night, many hours after the father has already left the house.

Mrs Braun had not mentioned anything about moving at the intake meeting or in the telephone support calls during the week preceding the second meeting. In this second meeting, essential information appears suddenly and dramatically. Even though the moving plan was certainly not new, Mrs Braun had not bothered to update the team. Although she had delivered lengthy, tedious descriptions of irrelevant behaviours during the intake, Mrs Braun neglected to mention this. When questioned about how this was possible, the mother answers casually that although this possibility came to light a long time ago, she failed to see the connection between the impending move and the intervention process. At this stage, Mrs Braun gives the impression that this is the first time that the issue of moving and the ensuing drama has ever occurred.

The day after the incident, Mary calls her mother at work, and asks if she can go out with her to a café after work to discuss the plan. When Mrs Braun comes home, Mary instigates a heated argument, accompanied by door slamming and locking herself in her room. In spite of this, shortly before the planned outing, she comes out of her room and reiterates her interest in going out with her mother. Mrs Braun employs her usual strategy of denial and bribery, suggesting, 'Let's go out and enjoy. Let's not talk about the move.'

However, Mary comes to the talk well prepared. She brings with her alternative ideas, whereby *she* can stay and live without having to move with her mother. Amongst those ideas, she even suggests moving to a residential facility which a friend of hers will be attending – anything to stay on familiar territory. Again, the mother employs another typical strategy, delaying the conversation to pacify Mary in the short term. Although she has no intention of entertaining any of Mary's suggestions, she promises that she will consider them carefully. Consistent with her deny-and-bribe strategy, Mrs Braun says, 'I don't mind *bribing* her. I even promised her that if she agrees to move, she will have a driver's licence and a car at the age of 16. Mary adamantly rejected my offer. *She is simply not mature enough to negotiate.*' Negotiations, according to Mrs Braun, are attempted bribery.

On their way home, Mary pushes her mother to respond to her suggestions. In spite of her promise that she would consider them carefully, her mother hastily responds, 'Yes, I've considered them and the answer is no.' An explosion erupts from which Mary cannot calm down. Upon arriving home she calls her father to verify the chances of intervening to change her mother's unbearable decree.

Mr Braun, who remained quiet until now, interjects here, 'Mary called me and said, "Dad, I want to ask you...are we moving or not?" I answered her that I think the family will move. She said, "I want you to know that if we move I will do something to myself!" and hung up the phone.' In the height of her distress, Mary believes that only a suicide threat can save her from this move. The father, for his part, believes that this issue can wait three whole days until his next scheduled visit with her. Mrs Braun adds here, 'Since then, I have hardly spoken to her at all.'

Mrs Braun does not volunteer information on the background of the moving issue. Only when the team pushes and asks if there was ever a similar outburst, does Mrs Braun answer hesitantly, in the affirmative. The father, on the other hand, states it clearly, 'Two similar crises were sparked by the prospect of possible moves to the US, the last of which happened six months ago.'

It appears that two years before, Mrs Braun raised the possibility of returning to the US. Mary opposed it vociferously, throwing major tantrums but at the same time raising legitimate objections: 'You are pressuring me and I don't know where I stand and where I will be.' Mary insists that this is the reason that she cannot concentrate on her studies. At a certain point, Mary tells her friends that she will be moving with her family to America. After months of hesitation, Mrs Braun shelves her plan and it drops from the agenda. Six months prior to the intervention, the plan resurfaces, bringing in its wake the same wave of violent opposition. Once again, she informs her friends of her planned departure and once again her mother shelves the idea. Her rationale: 'For Mary's sake and for mine.' At this point, the team finds out that her last therapy stint was initiated as a result of the last moving crisis.

At this point, Mr Braun offers his perspective: 'Mary and I had a strong and special relationship. There were things that Mary refused to let anyone else do for her — to bathe her, to cut her nails. Some nights she would come into our bed in the middle of the night, and we would throw her mother out of bed so that she could sleep alone with me.' However, lately this relationship has changed and Mary claims that her father is not on her side, insisting he is not her father anymore. Manipulating information, she pits one parent against the other. To the mother she will say, 'Dad said this and that about you' and *vice versa*. When that fails, she attacks her father's wife; even though according to the father, she has an excellent relationship with her replete with many long heart-to-heart talks. The father presumes that Mary prefers that the parents remain in dispute.

The better part of the meeting is dedicated to information gathering and to the attempt to establish clarity regarding the new facts that emerged during the session. The clashes and tantrums, whose source was unclear, now have a source as well as long history. Mrs Braun's tendency to deny and trivialize as the core reasons behind her confrontations with Mary is becoming clear.

The team examines the situation offering two different but closely related perspectives. From one perspective Mary appears to be an extremely abusive, aggressive, teen at risk, who employs extreme measures to gain attention. However, closer examination points to the fact that

anxiety lies at the core of her extreme behavour. The team elaborates
that anxiety may be the motivating force in the Braun family.

Anxiety, explains the team, has many faces but one nature. It tends
to lie behind loudness, rudeness, confrontation, provocation. Particularly in youth, it lies behind taking risks and the lack of motivation to
face achievements. As anxiety intensifies, the tendency to self-directed
aggression increases. At the same time, anxiety can also produce over-
activity. In the desire to find relief, other strategies, sometimes contradictory in nature, such as denial, ignoring, bribery and acting out, are
automatically put in motion. The more one employs these strategies,
the further one drifts from the solution; more fundamentally, the more
one employs these strategies the less able one is to actually identify
the anxiety and the reasons behind it. This explains not only Mary's
behaviour, but also Mrs Braun's trivialization of Mary's problem and
her engaging in the many different therapies she reported on.

The two languages in use in the Braun family represent ambivalence. Mrs Braun's position rings loud and clear, 'I am here but I am
there.' Although her physical presence and actions are here, all of her
energies are directed to another country. Her ongoing criticism of the
new place and culture lock her family into a state of isolation. Since
her stay in Germany is temporary, she also does not bother to cultivate
relationships. All of these impose a heavy burden on her and on her
children. Weakness becomes the weakness of the children. From this
perspective Mary desperately tries to set down roots in one place in
order to create an authentic identity that relates to her surroundings.
She demands continuity and stability that are so vital to her developing her own identity. From this perspective all Mary's manipulations,
and her loud and provocative behaviour, are designed to get help and
attention. Moreover, all her efforts are aimed at bringing her father
back. As in Mr Braun's description, Mary hopes that her father will
throw out her mother and his second wife from the virtual bed, for her
sake. The intimate closeness which Mr Braun describes is reduced to
weekly hour-long visits. It is not surprising that she feels betrayed and
abandoned, especially by the repeated plans of moving.

Here it is easy to identify how screaming and aggressiveness come
to cover fear and uncertainty. In Mary's perception of reality, the more
extreme her protest is, the more assured the father's attention and
presence is. Therefore, the team suggests at this stage that it is vital

and necessary for the parents to articulate a clear message to Mary. The suggested statements will form the declaration which should be carried out by the father. The declaration will put forward that:

- Mother and father will work together.
- Mother and father are in agreement regarding the fundamental issues that affect Mary's future and well-being.
- All acts and decisions regarding her will be the product of careful and responsible consideration.

Fundamental statements

It is about time that a fundamental statement (regardless of the planned move) needs to be stated by both parents to Mary as follows: 'It is true that your mother and father separated from one another. However, we did not separate from our joint responsibility to raise you and to care for you. Therefore, we have no dispute over the things that we permit and those that we forbid you to do. We will encourage anything that supports your well-being, and forbid whatever harms your welfare.'

The second element of the declaration should be as follows: 'Both of us can look at you children from the place of common interests. In spite of our differences of opinion, we share one clear common knowledge – that we are responsible to do everything in our power to improve our children's lives.'

The team suggests that these two statements will form the crux of the declaration that should be announced soon.

The third element of the declaration has to address Mary's repeated suicide threats: 'All of us (Mom, Dad and Dad's wife) agree that we cannot legitimize the loss of hope, we cannot remain silent in the face of your suicide threats. We stridently oppose statements such as "If not, I will commit suicide." Suicide is not an option, and we will do everything we can to protect you from thinking and speaking like this.'

The fourth element of the declaration will address the question of moving: 'Employment and sustenance for daily living is a fundamental way that we care for our children, even if our workplace demands that we move from one place to another. In this move we will be able to live closer to one another and it will enable me to be more present and involved in your life.'

Their fourth statement should state that they categorically oppose any type of verbal or physical abuse directed towards her brother, 'We have decided that we strongly oppose the way that you hurt your brother. We forbid you to do anything harmful to him like beating or cursing him. We intend to do all that we can to protect both of you from such behaviours…we will not give up on you or give in to you.'

Both parents react with hesitation. Mrs Braun is hesitant for two reasons, 'Won't it be confusing for Mary?' and 'Where are the sanctions?' she asks. The father expresses his reservations, 'I hope that it will not create a greater problem. I was hoping to convince her to agree to moving.' It is apparent that both parents are extremely uncomfortable with the idea of stepping forward together to announce the clear, authoritative statements suggested above. Here they are reminded that if they would like the situation ultimately to improve, they have to leave their comfort zone – they must abandon their old, ineffectual ways that involve lengthy debates and bribery. And again, the team stress, lengthy debates, bribery and inconsistency of plans, action and behaviour are the major contributors to confusion and uncertainty in life.

Explaining that that fear of change is very natural, the team encourages them to recognize and derive strength from the innate morality of this new approach. At the same time the team point out that it requires resilience and a great deal of patience. Instead of talking to their daughter as a best friend, they must talk to her from the position of loving, protective parents who tell their daughter: 'We recognize the confusion we brought into your life and we are sorry for it. We have made a firm decision that we will do all we can, to avoid creating confusion in the future. Our decisions henceforth will be made with careful consideration of your future and well-being…' Presented in this sequence and in this manner, even the most oppositional child can relate to such moral reasoning.

The session is sealed with the decision of how and when to make the declaration.

THE SECOND SESSION: ON SUSPICION, PROPORTIONS AND PRIORITIES

At the second session Mrs Braun appears alone, explaining that due to urgent issues at work, the father could not come.

In response to the team's perfunctory 'How are you?' she unleashes a slew of complaints about Mary's loitering at night. With a worried tone, she describes the latest incident in minute detail. In the context of the last session which centered around grave concern about Mary's suicide threats and the pending declaration, the mother talks about loitering as if it were the burning issue endangering her daughter.

A few directed questions reveal that perhaps the incident was not quite as dramatic as she describes. Mary, who was supposed to come home at 10.30pm, appears half an hour late, explaining that she preferred to walk home rather than take the bus. To the question of whether she had an idea of Mary's whereabouts, Mrs Braun answers: 'I knew exactly where she was.'

The team directs the discussion to the topic of proportionate worry and proportionate reactions in dealing with oppositional children, especially adolescents. For parents to act successfully they must evaluate the gravity of any given situation, exercise appropriate control over the child and then soothe the situation. The team suggests that Mrs Braun examines the incident bearing the following points in mind:

- She admitted herself that she knew exactly were Mary was.
- Mary was only half an hour late, an acceptable amount of time.
- Mary gave a reasonable explanation for her lateness.

In conclusion the team states that the term 'loitering' is inappropriate and disproportionate to what actually happened. At the same time, the team adds, Mrs Braun was right in making Mary aware that walking alone late at night is dangerous. The team highlights a significant shift – the obvious progress from the situation described at the intake, where Mary habitually disappeared into the night after her mother went to bed. Mrs Braun slowly calms down and agrees that she needs to integrate this new perspective. The rest of the session is dedicated to the declaration.

THE THIRD SESSION: THE DECLARATION

Two days prior to the declaration, both parents met to draft it, based on the team's advice and integrating the version offered by the team. The declaration is carried out in Mary's room. After the mother hands her the written form, the father reads it out loud. Though all signs seem to indicate its success, Mrs Braun is unhappy with the event for different reasons. She claims that the father was pressed for time and read the declaration too quickly, 'I could barely follow his reading... I hope Mary could follow it better...' As for Mary's response, 'There was no reaction, neither positive nor negative, just great surprise.' Afterwards, Mary agrees to go to a pre-arranged dinner with her father and 'comes back ready to move, understanding and loving..."I love you, Mom" she says...'

On control and uncertainty

Upon bringing Mary home, Mr Braun suggests that he and Mrs Braun meet again to discuss the grievances that Mary raised over dinner, at which point he hastily leaves to prepare for a meeting the next day. Mrs Braun is left feeling humiliated, as if she has been taken to task by him.

'I don't know what went on during that dinner,' she continues, 'Mary came back a different person – this is *very suspicious*. It could be that he made *big promises* to her that he will not be able to fulfil. That has happened many times in the past and *I'm afraid of it. I will be the one to get hurt*, it will just ricochet back at me. I'm afraid of her emotional blackmail and her manipulation. The dramatic declaration will not last long. Although Mary says she is ready to move, she is still hesitant. She told me, "I removed a heavy stone off your heart by consenting to move. I hope I'll get rid of my stone too."'

The team suggests that Mrs Braun should examine her reaction, specifically her uncertainty and suspicion regarding the exchanges between Mary and her father. The team reminds her that one can only control one's own actions and thoughts. In her case, she must develop faith in Mary's father's good intentions. Although Mr Braun may perceive the situation and the events differently, although he may have a different approach to Mary there are no grounds to believe that Mary's welfare is of lesser importance to him than to her. On the contrary, after being with her father, Mary returns appeased and ready to move, a goal to which they jointly aspired. The fact that Mr Braun asks that they discuss Mary's grievances is not only legitimate, but absolutely necessary. As an integral part of the pre-planned effort to de-escalate the situation, this discussion can improve the chances of negotiation of the best terms for all participants. Mary's hesitation, mentioned above, is perfectly natural. It indicates that she is ready to enter into a dialogue. This stands in direct contrast to her dead-end tactics of the past: the tantrums, the threats to harm herself, the never-ending debates.

It is only natural for Mary to feel pain and even grieve over the potential loss of her peer group and her familiar territory. The prospect of finding new friends and new territory seems to her insurmountable. The fact that the parents live apart is a reality and as such there will always be times where Mary is with one of her parents alone and shares with one and not the other. It is therefore the parents' responsibility to synchronize all shared information.

Mrs Braun claims that her reaction is one of caution; she says she is afraid to develop expectations that are doomed to fail. Mrs Braun explains her suspicions of Mary's manipulations and her suspicions of the father's ulterior motives as 'caution'. The team suggests that although caution is generally positive, it can be tricky. Caution, by its nature, prevents things from happening or taking their natural course. Very often avoidance can disguise itself as caution.

Adjusting expectations

After the team's feedback, Mrs Braun raises the school issue. Describing her search for a new school for Mary, she comments, 'The clock is ticking.' She is searching alone. 'I will involve Mary and her father;' her emphasis is on the future tense. Meanwhile, she reports, Mary's father's promise to send Mary to a school with a focus on music is putting pressure on her. 'The father says, "You must send her to a school that specializes in music, I've promised her"... However, I'm not sure that such a school exists, and I don't think that she will get in anyway... There he goes making pipe dream promises that I end up ruining...' The guidance counsellor at the school has already recommended that Mary attend a school that has a residential facility attached to it. Although she would be sleeping at home and not in the facility, she could benefit from much more personal attention as a day student. The drawbacks are that most of the students there come from difficult backgrounds and it is located far from the place to which they intend to move. As such, forging friendships will be difficult. Mrs Braun expresses her hesitation. 'How can I send Mary to a school with such a problematic population? How am I to make the right decision?'

The team responds by saying that although the school issue is an important one, putting so much emphasis on it diverts the focus from the important process that has been begun. Nevertheless, the team recommends that she should immediately involve Mary in the search for a new school. Mary must be aware of all the hesitations and concerns involved. In addition, she must hear whether she qualifies or not directly from whoever makes this decision and not from Mrs Braun. With this clarification, the team states that the current process is designed to create the proper perspective from which to monitor her child and to act as needed. In this sense, it is there to create within her the appropriate parental awareness that is independent of the ongoing drama.

The team points out that since the declaration, there are real signs that indicate that Mary is allowing her parents' right to navigate her life and at the same time reclaiming her natural role as their child. The team acknowledges that there are additional issues which cannot be ignored. Mary's underachievement requires special attention. It is also a fact that finding her a suitable school is a difficult task. For their part, the team encourages Mrs Braun to explore *all* possibilities, and they recommend that she consult with an expert in the field of special education. However, the most important thing, they stress, is that both parents must be ready and willing to adopt transparency from now on. From this perspective they should communicate the following message: 'Together, we must face the reality exactly as it is.' Here Mrs Braun suddenly bursts into tears and says: 'It is such a difficult reality for her. I want to protect her, but I can't.'

The team reassures her that although the situation is far from simple, it can be interpreted in a different light, especially her last comment. Rather than focusing on helplessness, the team encourages her to see the promise in telling her child, 'We are mobilizing all our resources to protect you... We are investing our best efforts into finding you a suitable school... We will do our best to help you to develop your musical talents in an appropriate framework... We will invest all of the time and attention necessary to see this through.' Although both parents must be ready to invest, Mrs Braun is told that she need not hesitate to operate alone in the event that the father does not co-operate.

Mrs Braun's statement 'It is difficult for me to tell Mary the truth' is of great importance as it is a clear expression of the confusion mentioned on a couple of occasions. The team points out that the antidote to that confusion is to talk about the things as they *are* rather than as they *should be*. Nevertheless, discussing reality as it is must be done delicately and gently. Viewing reality from a gentle place does not allow for crises to occur. One must be able to talk about the problems without falling apart – without Mrs Braun falling into despair and without Mary threatening suicide. It is a fact that when well-planned, pre-meditated statements were given to Mary without rage or excitement, Mary responded not in a crisis manner but with surprise, attentiveness and even agreement.

The session is closed with the recommendation that she continue the delicate work of communicating with the father and sharing the difficulties with him. Here again, the team re-emphasizes the importance and value of the father's co-operation. Full co-operation does not mean just informing him or entertaining the possibility of sharing information with him in the future, as she mentioned above. Sharing information is an ongoing process, here and now. The team emphasizes the importance of accepting the fact that each parent brings a quality which the other does not possess. In that context, Mary can keep calm, knowing that her two parents are dealing with her responsibly, each in their own way. This is the vital joint message which they must convey to Mary.

Mrs Braun shares with the team that on the coming Wednesday, during the father's regular visit, she and Mr Braun plan to meet without the children.

THE FOURTH SESSION: A BREAKTHROUGH

Mrs Braun shows up alone at the third session. Again, urgent matters at work prevented the father from joining. In addition, the conversation that was to take place between them on Wednesday did not materialize in the end. Yet, in spite of this, Mrs Braun appears for the first time smiling and at ease. When the team opens by announcing that it is the fourth session, she hastens to add that the time is flying by far too quickly and that there is still so much to do. Eager to tell the events of the passing week, she reports that the situation at home was quiet – the week had passed without any crises. She successfully avoided escalation and she managed to stop arguments and calm situations, thereby preventing them from becoming full-scale confrontations.

The team member responsible for the telephone support conversations presents his feedback. He reports that during this short period of time, Mrs Braun has improved the atmosphere at home and changed the tone of her exchanges with Mary. It seems that both mother and daughter have reached a better place. Indeed, Mrs Braun is employing the work principles of the Non-Violent Response Model, with significant results. However, before Mrs Braun continues her report of the successful week, he enlists the team's input and advice on a question that Mrs Braun raised in their last conversation.

Co-operation with Mary's father is the subject of her request. Although the father was prevented from joining her this time, in general he has shown willingness to co-operate. Moreover, in spite of her criticism and dire projections, she herself witnessed that he co-operated and conducted the declaration according to the given instructions. However, she is concerned that she is failing to communicate with him. She is aware of the fact that as far as he is concerned she sounds like she is forever complaining. Mrs Braun turns to the team for help in influencing him to be more active in the process.

The team decide to contact the father. Reframing her request again, the team summarizes her change of attitude by reflecting back to Mrs Braun her insights and her subsequent choices: 'The father is the most natural partner that we can have in this process. Mrs Braun wants his co-operation. He is her most natural supporter. She needs the team's support to draw him closer to the process.'

Encouraged by this, Mrs Braun continues the report of last week's success. On the school front, she consulted the special education expert recommended by the team. Following his recommendations, she set up several appointments for her and Mary to visit various schools and Mary has become an integral part of the school search effort. However, she reports a difficult incident which occurred in the last week. Since the only computer at home is in Mary's room, Mrs Braun describes entering the room in her absence to check email, only to be met with a strong stench of cigarette smoke and an ashtray full of cigarette butts. Later, after picking Mary up from a friend, she confronts Mary with the fact that she has broken the 'No smoking in the house' agreement. Mary begins to scream and shout, vehemently protesting the invasion of her privacy. She repeats 'You have no right to enter my room' all the way home. All the while, Mrs Braun maintains her silence. Shortly after arriving home, Mary comes to her mother and says, 'I'm sorry. I overreacted. I won't smoke in the house anymore and you can come into my room any time you want.' The team congratulates Mrs Braun on her superb implementation of de-escalation as described in the *Guidebook for Parents*.

Magnified worries

Mrs Braun's anxious tone resurfaces. Her success does not seem to reduce or calm anxiety. In addition, she appears to be incapable of making a distinction between severe and common problems – all of them seem to be of the same magnitude. She begins to talk about how worried she is about Mary's smoking. Did the father's smoking in front of Mary have a negative effect on her? Did the fact that she herself used to smoke influence Mary? Mrs Braun does not wait for answers, negating this concern on the premise that she started smoking when she was much older than Mary.

The team asks Mrs Braun to pause and observe her tendency to magnify her worries. In doing so, she allows those worries to overshadow the subtle successes that she has begun to achieve. She is reminded once again that two weeks ago, we spoke of a girl that shook her home with abusive language, terrorizing and terrifying her brother and threatening suicide. Now, this same girl expresses her regret within a short period of time, for relatively minor outbursts. She consents to the 'No smoking in the house' rule and allows her mother free access to her room. These are major achievements and it would be a pity to allow those to dissolve under the force of excess worries, which although legitimate are minor, compared to the original problems.

The team asks her to consider the difference in children now and in the past. There are many things that children of this generation indulge in, which we as 14-year-olds would never have dreamed of. Times have changed and with them, smoking, piercing and the like, have become symbols of being 'cool' and belonging to a social circle. The only choice left for parents is to state definitively: 'We object to smoking' – period! In the same spirit the team suggests that she invest her effort efficiently – only where it is likely to reap rewards. Preventing Mary from smoking is a losing battle and is thus not worth her energy. At the same time, she must make a statement regarding the dangers of smoking – the fact that it damages the health of the smoker as well as those who are subjected to second-hand smoke. Therefore, the house is off limits for smoking. The statement that emerges from here is as follows: 'Although I accept you the way you are, I cannot and will not encourage habits that I object to. I will not stand and watch you with indifference while you inflict harm upon yourself. You cannot make such a demand of me.' This argument, when reiterated constantly, remains solid against any type of argument or pressure.

Mrs Braun's next comment concerns Mary's piercing. Apparently, after the declaration and the subsequent dinner discussion with her father, Mary came home and removed the piercing from her eyebrow. To her astonished mother she said, 'I had enough of it.' Two days later she put it in again, this time saying, 'I can't afford the "good girl" stigma.' Mrs Braun summarizes that smoking and piercing reflect Mary's need to belong to a group – even if it is 'the bad kids society'.

The team suggests she should examine her perspective carefully. One approach would be that Mary excuses her low achievement by convincing herself that high achievement belongs to nerds, and that being a nerd is negative. Therefore, she chooses to wear all the signs, such as smoking and piercing, that identify her with what is considered cool.

However, another way to look at it would be as follows. Mary has developed a real resistance to Mrs Braun's high and at times unrealistic expectations of Mary and of herself. Mary, in her rebellious behaviour, is demonstrating clearly that she wants no part of that. Yet, at the same time, when Mary attempts to mainstream her behaviour, she finds herself trapped socially. Removing her piercing for example, renders her an outsider in her peer group. Such an understanding calls for the decision that rather than focusing on piercing and smoking, Mrs Braun's efforts should be invested in containing and supporting Mary to move to a better place. How to do this in a gentle yet effective manner requires much thought and careful planning.

This context provides an ideal setting to raise the school issue, particularly the issue of placing Mary in a school whose student body comprises primarily students from troubled backgrounds. In Mary's case, there is no choice but to go to such a school. At the same time, the Brauns must invest intention and effort in creating and opening up social alternatives for Mary outside of school. She must have other places and groups with which to interact, for example where she can learn music or perhaps a gym facility to materialize her long-standing desire to exercise seriously. Mary's meeting different and new people and being woven into different new places must be the next item on the immediate agenda of the Braun family.

THE LAST SESSION: ON THE IMPORTANCE OF SOCIAL NETWORKS

After filling in the battery of questionnaires, Mrs Braun enters the session smiling and looking pleased. Not waiting for any introduction from the team, she says that although it might sound awkward, she must begin with a confession. 'I have made a mistake. For a long time already, Mary has asked me to get together with her friend and her friend's mother. Although you strongly advised me to take advantage of such opportunities, I never responded appropriately to this offer. I've consented again and again, only to forget about it all over again. But Mary is very serious about it. Yesterday, she raised the issue again. Apparently, a group of kids and their parents meet regularly, to spend leisure time together. Although now I see it in a positive light, the only question is how to proceed with it, with the moving date so near.' Continuing she says, ' I have always had a problem with official bodies – school, teachers, counsellors. I have failed totally. In each encounter with the "system", I've created strong antagonism against me. It is so difficult for me that I have practically given up...and now...I am afraid...'

Mrs Braun stops in mid-sentence, pausing for the first time, looking deeply sad. New social prospects and old failures – antagonistic encounters with officials – melt into one. She does not recall any ordinary, informal social relationships – only those with officials. Although already in the first session we had recommended that she should build a social network, only now has it crystallized into an insight, only now has the penny dropped. Only in the last session, does Mrs Braun reach a point where she finds herself truly accountable. It is the beginning of an understanding that the answers to the issues facing the Brauns lie in her – not in Mary's underachievement and dramatic reactions and not in the father's lack of understanding of the situation nor in his willingness to co-operate.

The team helps Mrs Braun to see Mary's request as an invitation to step into a social network. It is an invitation to abandon her distant attitude towards people. Mary is communicating to her how necessary it is that her mother becomes a full participant in her environment. Participation, for Mary, implies the longed-for approval. Mary needs her mother to step in and take a clear stand that states unambiguously, 'This is our home. This is where we live.'

The team encourages Mrs Braun to take the chance. With the time and effort that she has invested in the intervention, she has initiated important changes which have produced tangible results. So far she has implemented the tools at her disposal wisely. The next step that lies ahead of her, must be to gain new experiences, to come into contact with new people, to forge new relationships and integrate them into her life. The more involved she and her children are in real relationships, the less violence and crises will dominate their family's life. As for her encounters with officials, they must be understood in the same manner. All the intervention's principles that she applied so successfully in the family setting, can be applied to her interactions with officials. To list a few: planned, pre-meditated action, defining exceptions, listening, choosing battles, correct timing, being well informed, respect for others, transparency. When these principles are implemented, escalation and antagonism cannot take over the interaction, be it with officials or with any other social contacts.

Mrs Braun is reminded again of Mary's portrait as given by her when first contacting us. The wild and uncontrolled girl she described at the first two sessions, has calmed down. The atmosphere at home has changed. Her relationship with her brother has changed for the better; she no longer attacks him as she used too.

As in other systems, a first step, a small initial change, sets off a chain of reactions. Here Mrs Braun comments: 'If you check my MHI now (the mental health questionnaire that rates well-being), you will notice a substantial difference from my answers at the beginning of the intervention. The situation has totally changed; our home is simply not the same home. Also, I was miserable at work in the past and now I am happy with my new job.'

The team gives credit to Mrs Braun for her co-operation, especially her close work with the team member who conducted the telephone support calls. 'I could not have done it without him.' With him she encountered, perhaps for the first time, a new experience different from her past negative encounters with other officials. During his well-planned, reliable and consistent contact, he helped her to economize her words, as well as moderate and reformulate her responses to the daily crises occurring at home.

The team closes the session with a warm recommendation that Mrs Braun keep up the good work of enlisting Mary's father as her supporter. Reminding her that she must develop a generous attitude towards him, the team urges her to make space for him. This can be achieved by conveying the message to him that she acknowledges his distinctive place and relationship with his children. From now on, she will not try to deny, undermine or negate his understanding of his kids and his influence on them. Agreeing with these assertions, Mrs Braun adds, 'I have always known it. The question is only how strong I am at that moment.' The team reassures her that as they emphasized many times before, she now has a set of tools to strengthen her in dealing with the situation. It is her choice to implement them – she is no longer as ignorant as she thought she was. If a relapse occurs, she can always consult the *Guidebook for Parents*.

During this session, Mrs Braun describes her thoughts and feelings eloquently, in a well-organized and efficient manner. She is ready to face her accountability for the failures of the past. She is ready to apply the new concepts, insights and experience gained through the process. Indeed, she is ready to take these to the next level – to test them outside the structure of intervention. The team suggests that their joint work on Mary's conduct and the relations with her, has brought other critical issues, that go far beyond Mary, to the surface. It has opened Mrs Braun's eyes to see matters and materials beyond the targets set by the intervention. Defining and reframing these unspoken issues has provided her with significant relief.

With these words, the fifth session and the intervention come to an end. In another four weeks we will meet Mrs Braun for a follow-up session.

THE FOLLOW-UP: THE CHALLENGE

It has been four weeks since we have last seen Mrs Braun. She shows up to the session looking extremely tired, joking that she will need another eight hours in order to get into the swing of things. The follow-up session is designed to find out whether the changes which occurred during the intervention have been maintained. It begins with filling out a battery of questionnaires.

Mrs Braun reports that she continues to implement the principles she learned during the intervention. She claims that Mary is responding well to her. 'There is no essential change at school, but the atmosphere at home continues to be good.' She assumes that partially, the good atmosphere at home is due to the fact that she is less present at home and so she nags the children less. However, she notices a real deterioration in the children's relationships with their father. He has not kept up his weekly meetings and he has stopped paying alimony complaining of having difficulties. Apparently, the father is going through major financial problems: 'He had financial problems in former times too, but in the past six years he has never missed a payment.' Stressed, he does not state that he is not interested in seeing the children, he just cancels at the last minute, leaving the anticipating kids disappointed and hurt. He keeps up the weekends visits only because 'I insist on maintaining them.' At present, she takes them to him, because otherwise he would not meet them at all. Mrs Braun is convinced that he would prefer not to have them at all for the weekends. Now that they have begun to talk about it, she is finally beginning to get a clearer picture and understand the situation. To her surprise, she discovered that the kids were not feeling comfortable in their father's home. Mary explains that her father spends most of the weekend sleeping, while his wife criticizes her. Only now does she understand the extent of Mary's suffering.

The team emphasizes that now that she has established a stronger, deeper dialogue with her children, it has opened up the possibility of her awareness of issues that she did not know about or notice in the past. The question remains, what should be done with the new information at hand? The situation may be temporary, yet she must still be equipped with the appropriate response should it persist. At the same time, she must be careful about forcing the visits on the kids or on their father. It would be wise to give the father time to recuperate and sort out his difficulties.

Her aim should be to help the kids understand the situation, rather than reinforce their belief that they are unwanted. This understanding is critical for the future, since as she herself maintains, he has never before neglected his responsibility towards his children. The team reminds her again of the importance of maintaining a dialogue with the father, emphasizing the idea that even a very limited dialogue is better than no dialogue at all. They encourage her to exercise understanding and compassion for his apparent difficulties.

Mrs Braun continues her report. Referring to the challenges faced in the last month, she says: 'There were different, smaller crises during the past month. Phone calls came in from Mary's school concerning problems of one kind or another. I stopped co-operating with the school. It is a lost cause this year. I want to find a school that will be a good partner, but I have not yet found an apartment. I need to work on myself in order to have good relations with the next school. I realize how resentful I am towards the school. I hope that it is the school's failure and not mine.' Summarizing, she says, 'This has been such a difficult year, worse than any year that I can remember.'

She entertains the idea of keeping Mary back a grade. If that happens, Mary will be one year older than the others. The fact that she is less mature than the others will not be 'as apparent as it is now'. However, when the idea is mentioned to Mary, she instinctively rejects it. Mrs Braun tries to convince her but then stops, realizing that it would be best if she let Mary mull it over herself: 'I told her that it is an option and I asked her to think about it and consider it. Since then, I have not raised the subject again. Although I think it is a good idea, I prefer that she choose this solution on her own rather than me imposing it on her.'

The team elaborates here on the idea of creating a 'pause' in order to re-route Mary from her familiar path to failure. Since the drama has been removed from the situation, there is now room to pause and entertain new ideas. Repeating the last grade, while providing her with the necessary support, seemed positive. It could afford her the opportunity to develop proper discipline and work habits.

Does Mrs Braun feel stronger and up to the many challenges ahead of her? She answers positively: 'Yes, I am surprised at myself. The shouting, the tantrums, the cursing and the terror; they are all gone. Strange. It is not that we have solved the problems, but somehow everything is different. Mary has matured so much in the last month. She has not bothered, taunted, cursed or hit her brother in weeks. I surprised Mary with tickets for a rock concert, performed by a group that I know she adores. I could never bring myself to initiate such a gesture in the past. I allowed her to choose a new musical instrument and it is amazing to watch her enthusiasm. She is passionately participating in her drum lessons. I know that it has only been four weeks so maybe it is premature to get too excited about it. I even noticed that there are some new kids who are seeking contact with her. Although I like the idea of getting together with other moms, now that every minute of mine is planed in advance, technically I have not been able to pull it off. I'd like to pursue this once we establish ourselves in the new city. I like this direction.' Mrs Braun adds, 'I have the feeling that I'm going to need to employ the same tools with my son. He is only 11 but I notice that he is beginning adolescence. He is starting to rebel, albeit not as strongly as Mary...' She summarizes her answer by saying, 'I think that we have achieved the goals we set for ourselves.'

It is time for the team to congratulate Mrs Braun on her dedicated efforts in creating a new dialogue with Mary. It is time to acknowledge the new perspective on life that she has adapted. It is clearly apparent that the same events and difficulties are losing their heavy, dramatic effect. Instead of drama, there is contemplation, assessment and planning.

The team reminds her of the challenging work that lies ahead of her. Mrs Braun is encouraged to pursue it with the following understandings: the certainty that she is more knowledgeable than she was before she began the intervention; the knowledge that she possesses tools to identify and overcome new obstacles; and the knowledge that she is indeed no longer in the desperate position she was in when we first met her.

CHAPTER EIGHT

Family and Community

The referral call was initiated by the mother, Mrs Halpern, who is in her mid-forties and a secretary by profession. She presents herself as a housewife and is a single mother of ten children. Six months prior to her call, she was suddenly widowed and at that point, her family reached breaking point. She complains of deep distress and extreme difficulties with the nine children presently living at home. Manifestations of violence, severe outbursts, and a lack of boundaries are especially marked amongst two of her children – 16-year-old Daniel and seven-year-old Asher.

THE INTAKE SESSION: THE FIRST STAGE

The Halpern family, a Haredi[1] family, lived for a period in England. At the time, the father was an extremely wealthy international businessman and established himself as a leader in his community, as well as a benefactor of the poor. Typically, he would host two hundred guests at his Sabbath table. The mother was active in charitable causes, while at the same time managing her home and raising her children with the assistance of professional staff.

After a prosperous period, the father's business crashed and he was besieged by creditors and the tax authorities. His holdings were seized and he was charged with embezzlement. A short time before the verdict was reached, the father decided to leave the country together with his wife and children, without taking leave of anybody. The family

---

1   Haredi: a term that describes ultra-orthodox Jews.

leaves carrying a few personal items and the children are simply told that they are going on vacation to Antwerp where the father's family resides.

Upon arrival in Antwerp they move into a tiny apartment in a poor section of the city and the family is sustained by charity. The father sinks into a deep depression and during this period, intense quarrelling erupts between the couple. Mr Halpern claims that his wife withheld her support during the crisis. Mrs Halpern's attempts to seek external help and psychological advice are met with anger and suspicion. He accuses her of attempting to humiliate him and even betray him. Forcing her into silence, he communicates with her tersely through the children, only on practical matters. A year after a short, failed attempt at reconciliation, the father leaves home and returns to his mother's house. He consents to his children's visits less and less and files for divorce.

The mother, who kept hoping for reconciliation, experiences a serious breakdown and is not able to take care of her kids. At that point, the kids act as their own masters. On a Sabbath visit to their father, during prayers at the synagogue, the father suffers a heart attack and dies instantly. Six months later, the mother initiates the referral for help.

Although Mrs Halpern is close to her two sisters, they can only provide her with limited support as they are dealing with large families of their own. From the time of her husband's death, both his family and his many friends sever relations with the bereaved family. Mrs Halpern finds herself confronted by his extended family who reject her, claiming that she brought about the death of their son. The heavy debt and disputed joint property serve as a further excuse to ostracize the mother, whom they refuse to see or accept as their son's widow. The father's family agrees to have the grandchildren visit, yet only selectively without any explanation. At the same time, they deliberately cultivate a special relationship with Daniel, who bears a striking physical resemblance to his father. The only child to say Kaddish,[2] Daniel holds on tightly to his father's memory, to the extent that he even wears his father's clothes. Together with his father's family, he bears marked hostility to his mother, claiming that she stole his

---

2   Kaddish: the prayer recited by a mourner for eleven months, after the loss of a loved one.

father's life. Slowly, Mrs Halpern finds herself alienated from her late husband's family and from her community.

In the Haredi community, it is a taboo to tarnish the father's image by presenting him as a person who not only failed in his business dealings but also betrayed the trust of many. The rift between the mother and father is a taboo as well. The family's abrupt departure in the middle of the night, the father's sudden departure from home, the mother's retreat into silence and the father's decision to divorce – none of those issues are discussed with or explained to the children. Outside the family, however, the rumour mill begins to spin and Daniel is the one who brings these rumours home. Although he is careful with the first taboo, he challenges the second one. In his every encounter with his mother, he calls her terrible names in front of his brothers, challenging her right to be called the wife of his father and as such, the head of the household. The brothers pretend that none of this is happening. Paradoxically, the mother continues to invest much of her energy – even after the father's death and despite the harsh attacks of her son Daniel and her late husband's family – to protect his memory as a benevolent philanthropist.

The ten children are torn between their loyalty to their mother and their loyalty to their father and his family. During this period, the children display a wide range of symptoms: depression, not being able to wake up in the morning for work or school, intolerable physical and verbal outbursts, and tantrums amongst the younger children. The impact of the ongoing events leaves its strongest mark on Daniel, the 16-year-old.

At the point of referral, the family had just moved to a larger apartment yet Mrs Halpern still maintains her household without any outside help. Although she complains of utter despair, she manages to keep the problems at home a carefully guarded secret – even from the social worker assigned to her family. Towards the community, she puts up a front and is extremely anxious about exposing her children's mis-behaviour, as well as their breaches in religious observance. She feels that all of these will inevitably bring her under harsh scrutiny and criticism as an incompetent mother and will serve to strengthen the claims against her, which were also the basis of the father's decision to divorce her. Her weak link with the community is combined with her sense of humiliation stemming from the radical change from the powerful, wealthy woman to the woman who is dependent on charity. Although she does not experience public censure directly, in Daniel's moments of fury, the rumours that are circulating on the outside come lashing out at her.

Even though she professes to feel deep distress in dealing with almost all of her children (aside from the two youngest), Mrs Halpern manages to highlight their good character traits and their unique abilities and talents. In her accounts of family life, there is ample evidence of signs of affection among them, in spite of their extremely difficult situation.

Profile of a family in distress

The following is a short description of the members of the Halpern family.

One of the family members, a 22-year-old son, lives and works abroad. The mother has regular phone contact with him.

Jona, 20, is deeply depressed and unable to get up for work. He has shed religious observance: he smokes in the house on the Sabbath,[3] does not wear a head cover or Tefillin[4] and does not pray regularly. The mother, who insists on keeping the stringently religious way of life which the family has always kept, is deeply disturbed by his behaviour. She feels that the community will attribute his rebellion to her inadequacy as a mother.

Daniel is 16 and, taller and more mature than his age, has always been very serious. Strikingly similar to his father in appearance and character, he was deeply connected to him from a young age. After his death, Daniel establishes a website as a tribute to his father's memory, expresses physical and verbal violence to his mother, and inspires terror amongst his siblings upon his arrival home for the weekends. Despite his extreme hostility towards her, his mother describes him as intelligent, polite to others and popular amongst his friends. Even though he lacks interest in religious studies and wants to leave the yeshiva,[5] the yeshiva has no complaints against him.

---

3   Sabbath: Saturday – the seventh day of the week and a day of rest. Jewish law prohibits any work-related activities on the Sabbath.

4   Tefillin: phylacteries – box-like appurtenances that accompany prayer, worn by Jewish adult males at the weekday morning services.

5   Yeshiva: an academy where Jewish religious texts are studied. At the high school level, yeshiva students generally board there as well.

Aaron, a pleasant 14-year-old, shows signs of emotional distress and behaves in a depressed manner. He has trouble waking up for school; he falls asleep during lessons and has difficulties in concentrating on his studies.

Shulem, a 12-year-old, a gentle and quiet child, also has trouble getting up in the morning. Amongst all the children, he is picked on and humiliated most by his brother Daniel.

Esther, ten years old, shows signs of mental and emotional developmental delay compared to her age group. Although she suffers from motor problems and poor language skills, she goes to an ordinary religious school.

David, a nine-year-old, loveable, energetic and argumentative child, does not wake up in the morning and refuses to accept authority – at home or at school. A partner in crime with his younger brother Asher, he willingly participates in the plots that Asher initiates.

Asher, seven years old, is described as an intense child who, from the time that he was a baby, has always demanded undivided attention. His reaction to lack of attention manifests itself in incessant screaming, hitting his younger brothers and breaking objects at hand. Among his favourite pastimes are lighting fires and climbing up to forbidden high locations. Every morning begins with a tantrum. Initially, he refuses to get up and when he eventually does, he does not pull himself together in time to catch his school bus. While at school, he refuses to listen to the teacher's instructions, leaves the classroom without permission, climbs on his desk during class, disrupts the lessons, refuses to participate in mandatory morning prayers and generally busies himself with bothering those around him. On weekends, he clashes strongly with his brother Daniel, and 'loves to be his victim', according to his mother.

Eliezer, five years old, and Malka, four years old, are the victims of their brother Asher.

The intervention goals
From the mother's account it became apparent that the fundamental objective must be to restore the mother's position as the head of the family. This is a contested status, due to the family history and also due to the fact that the Haredi world attributes a less central status to the wife and demands modesty and reserve from widows, especially within the context of public community life.

Two ideal candidates, suited to work according to the model, are identified. Daniel and Asher, together and apart, display violent behaviour and are constant partners in escalation and loss of control in the family. However, only one can be chosen as the focus of the intervention. This choice is ultimately dictated by the requirements of the research project. Asher fits the criteria, while Daniel does not. Daniel studies in yeshiva and returns home only on the weekends, therefore it is impossible to keep telephone records on his escalating behaviour during the week. As such, it is decided that the treatment will focus on Asher, aged seven.

At the end of the intake session two goals are set:

• to minimize Asher's rage outbursts

• to restore Mrs Halpern's status as the head of the family.

The *Guidebook for Parents* is handed to Mrs Halpern and she is asked to read it thoroughly before the next session. She leaves the intake session with the team's promise that the intervention can be performed even without the children's participation. The team recommends that from now on, she should focus her attention on Asher and practise adopting and implementing the work principles. Ultimately, this will serve as the groundwork for more comprehensive work in the future with Daniel as well as the other problems facing this family.

THE FIRST SESSION: LOSING CONTROL

In the first therapeutic session after the intake session, the mother raises serious concern about the possible impact of her depressed son Jona on the other family members. Likewise, she expresses her concern about the tyrannical behaviour of her son Daniel, upon his return on the weekends. In addition, when Daniel comes home, her son Asher's violent acts intensify. The team reassures her that her work with Asher can be seen as a preliminary exercise, designed to ultimately enable her to cope with Daniel.

The following incidents taken from the first week's follow-up phone calls, demonstrate the principles in action.

Refusal and threat

In the attempt to identify her patterns of reaction to outbursts and tantrums, Mrs Halpern reports that her efforts to discipline her children are characterized by wordy exchanges. Lengthy explanations turn into arguments, which turn into threats of punishment. At the core of these incidents there can be: a TV programme, the use of the computer, a toy, a food item, the desire to leave the house at an unreasonable hour, refusal to do home work or lighting a fire in the house or in the yard. Seldom does she succeed in calming and pacifying Asher. Most of the time, her explanations and exhortations slide into screaming and then into punitive measures. Inevitably, she loses control to the point that she even hits him. These incidents leave a short-lived impression on Asher, after which he goes right back to his old ways.

The team points out to her two different types of escalations that are clearly present in the scenario that she describes: those of demands and those of hostility.

- Escalation of demands: in order to maintain peace, she gives in to Daniel but this only serves to increase his demands. For example, she denies the other children's access to the computer from the moment that he arrives home, in order to cater to his demands. Yet, he then makes additional monetary demands, which she simply cannot meet.

- Escalation of hostility: at the end of a shopping trip, Mrs Halpern is about to return home. Asher refuses to come back with her. All of her pleas fall on deaf ears. He is intractable in his refusal and taunts her by saying: 'What will you do to me if I don't return?' In response, the mother resorts to threats: 'If you don't come with me immediately, I will not let you into the house.' The child persists, returning home many hours after nightfall. In the meantime, the mother combs the neighbourhood to find him with no success. This incident demonstrates a typical exchange between her and Asher – her request, his refusal, her attempts to persuade, his taunts followed by her threats and resulting in an intensified escalation.

Here, the therapeutic dialogue attempts to demonstrate the reasoning by which the oppositional and coercive child functions. The team emphasizes to the mother that while she is focused on getting a result, such as getting her son home, the child is interested in the negotiation process with her. For the child, this negotiation is an attempt to push her outside the limit and define a new boundary. At the same time, the interaction serves an additional purpose – it is the child's way to get the attention he craves. The emotional force created by these interactions acts as a substitute for the feeling of arousal that should normally be supplied by containment and affection. As demonstrations of the latter are few and far between, the child's craving is satisfied by creating these substitutes time and again.

On the other hand, this also serves as an excellent example of an empty threat and the child's (very successful) attempt to take it to its furthest limit. At this point, the mother recognizes that the threat strategy is a trap for both her and her child. The conclusion emerging from this is that from now on, she will set limits using a few choice words, rather than her characteristic long-winded attempts at persuasion, threats and vows to punish. She is encouraged to repeat to herself: 'I react and respond irrespective of whether or not I attain my desired result.'

Identifying the sources of escalation

In the follow-up telephone calls, the mother recognizes that many times due to stress and overwork, she is short tempered. At these times, she shouts rather than speaks. As she begins to contemplate and process the new concepts she has learned and then reflect on what is actually happening in her home, she realizes that the problematic incidents overpower her best intentions. For example, after a terrible fight with her son Daniel, Asher approaches her for something that she apparently had promised him. While he unrelentingly demands her attention, refusing to be pushed off, she reacts by totally losing control and hitting him. Consequently, Asher runs away from home.

With the team's help, the mother begins to notice how closely her reactions resemble her child's. Moments of helplessness are accompanied by responses that are at once violent and child-like. During these moments, she forfeits her role as the adult. The team emphasizes to her that it is the adult who must take the initiative in this dynamic, by rising above the childish oppositional behaviour. It is the adult who must set higher standards for himself, which in this case are the standards of the principles of Non-Violent Resistance.

In the first therapeutic session the first assigned exercise is designed:

- to recognize escalatory situations with her son Asher, identifying what sparks them, how they work and assessing their varying levels of intensity
- to withhold and prevent herself from reacting in her usual way
- to substitute her old response with a new one based on the operative principles.

The therapeutic dialogue will continue:

- to recognize and validate the mother's suffering
- to help the mother abandon the perception of herself as a 'victim'
- to adapt and integrate the principles of the Non-Violent Resistance Model
- to offer moral support based on the reasoning of the model
- to help her overcome feelings of guilt while questioning the need to find a guilty party
- to assist her in overcoming rage and despair that are likely to recur.

THE SECOND SESSION: IDENTIFYING AND REFRAMING ESCALATORY DYNAMICS

In the second week, the discussion on the topics mentioned above deepens. A great deal of introspection is apparent on the part of Mrs Halpern, both on the behaviour in her home and on her contribution to intensifying the escalatory incidents which she describes. At this stage, the team helps her define these reflections as the beginning of a whole new understanding. These first glimpses spark further reflection on Asher's constant attacks on his younger brothers. Typically, the mother's reaction to these attacks involves shouting, threatening, locking Asher in the bathroom with corporal punishment following

A NON-VIOLENT RESISTANCE APPROACH WITH CHILDREN IN DISTRESS

closely behind. In addition, Mrs Halpern observes that most of the time, she is not actually present at the scene of the attack: 'Somehow it happens when I'm not around or when my attention is diverted.'

Mrs Halpern adopts a new response. When Asher physically attacks his siblings, she immediately goes to protect them. The first step is complete physical separation. Then in clear, terse language, she clarifies to them that under no circumstances will she permit this violence, adding that she must carefully consider how she will respond to the incident. At the same time, she constantly works at restraining herself from losing control, physically or verbally.

This position is built on a therapeutic discussion touching on the issue of guilt and the issue of shame. Together with the team, the mother raises the possibility of her feeling guilty that she is unable to supply sufficient protection to her children, as well as feeling shame that perhaps the outside world will find out about it. When violence is not dealt with openly and directly, it feeds on itself and provides fertile ground for future abuse. The team explains that through her violent reactions, she not only forfeits her role as the adult, but also presents a negative role model for the child who is being hit. The team shows the close connection between the feeling of parental helplessness and the phenomenon of inter-sibling violence. The mother's lack of physical and emotional presence not only increases the likelihood of such incidents, but also increases the danger inherent in them. Likewise, the team raises the link that the research field and clinical experience attribute to death, that being the loss of the father and the development of a taboo surrounding inter-sibling violence. All of these issues play a distinct role in her family's history, thus creating the high levels of dissonance and violence that characterize not only her reactions, but also those of other family members.

The team then instructs the mother to obstruct Asher's violence against his siblings and to suggest alternative reactions to those situations.

THE THIRD SESSION: PACIFYING THE SITUATION

For the first time since she became a widow, the mother establishes direct contact with the schools of each of her children. To her surprise, Asher's teachers report an improvement, the source of which is unclear. David, who until now spent a considerable amount of his

118 \

time at school loitering in the halls, has returned to the classroom. Asher's behaviour is calmer and Aaron and Shulem are more attentive in class.

The first support call of the week focuses on Asher's angry outbursts, his running wild and disrupting other people's affairs. In the past, this behaviour always caused the mother to lose control. Now, she is reminded that she is to maintain the principle of 'not being drawn in'; she is not to scream nor threaten. Instead, she must respond quietly and clearly, setting limits concisely. The mother reports that the ongoing supervision and guidance on Asher's case has heightened her consciousness of how she behaves towards her other children. She begins to notice that often when she is short tempered, she automatically slides into screaming. Now, after such incidents, she apologizes to her children and they occur less frequently. She returns to the third session encouraged by the results and suggests the possibility (that is impossible to actualize within the given structure of the intervention) of following up on each child and partnering him with his own personal coach.

Most of the work with Asher focuses on identifying those sequences when Asher 'invites' her into an escalatory confrontation. These sequences require special vigilance and caution on her part. If she is able to catch that critical moment – that is the optimal time to step in and influence the situation and the mood of the child. Indeed, if she succeeds at heading it off, possible intervals of communication open up which she can fill with affection and reconciliation.

The mother now attempts more frequently to create opportunities to express affection towards Asher: to stroke his head when he passes by, to give him compliments such as 'You have a terrific sense of humour!', to praise him when he finishes his food or completes any other assignment. Even on days when the school has called to inform her that he behaved badly, she asks him how he is feeling upon his return from school.

Parallel to these gestures, two goals are added to the exercise:

- getting Asher up in the morning on time
- stopping Asher from endangering himself and others (for example, running away, climbing up to dangerously high places, setting fire to things).

Brain-storming with the team, pre-bedtime habits are defined and these include preparing clothes and a sandwich for school the next day. Mrs Halpern will strive to organize this calmly and smoothly, without getting thrown off by Asher's pre-bedtime arguments, tantrums or outbursts. Likewise, she will strive to wake him up personally in the morning in a loving and pleasant manner. Again, her conduct towards him cannot in any way be coloured by the previous day's misbehaviour.

This switch between passivity and activity is marked by an original idea. Mother and son will engage in a special joint activity – preparing a bonfire. This will achieve three goals at the same time. First, the mother will remove the confrontation element as Asher is not allowed to play with fire. Second, she will be able to spend individual time with her son, in an activity that will 'fire' his imagination. Finally, she will actualize her obligation to supervise, clarifying to her son that dealing with fire can only be done under adult supervision.

The discussion deepens during the follow-up support calls, and moves towards the next objective: the sit-in. This exercise contains the critical element of mobilizing public opinion and support. During this week, the mother schedules two sit-ins – one with the younger children and one with the older children. During the sit-in in Asher and David's room, the mother is accompanied by an avrekh.[6] During the sit-in in Shulem and Aaron's room, she is accompanied by her sister. Asher and David react by bursting into laughter and playing wildly on their beds. Throughout the sit-in's 20-minute duration, the mother maintains silence. The sit-in ends when David suggests preparing snacks the night before for the following morning and being woken up with a specific song. As the older kids are naturally more even-tempered, the sit-in in their room passes by quietly and uneventfully. They also agree upon an earlier bedtime, with a request for hot chocolate in bed in the morning. How simple!

At this stage, there is a growing awareness that all of their current efforts are in effect a preparation and introduction to an even greater effort that their family reality requires.

---

6   Avrekh: a mature yeshiva student who can sometimes act as a 'big brother' to children in need.

THE FOURTH SESSION: MOBILIZING PUBLIC OPINION

By the third week, it becomes clear that it is time to elevate the intervention to the next level by redefining the central problem. From here on, the work revolves around the idea that the family's stability is dependent upon restoring the mother's place at the top of the family pyramid. This return to its 'natural state' can happen only when: (a) the family function like a micro-community, that is all family members must assume mutual responsibility towards one another; (b) the family reintegrate into the community, which can be achieved by resorting to the time-honoured tradition of mutual support so fundamental to the Haredi community.

The present period of counselling stresses the need for a massive mobilization of public opinion. This is designed to supply the support necessary to maintain the goals of the intervention, in spite of the daily difficulties and the number and complexity of the problems with which this family has to deal. Parallel to this, the mother exercises daily the principle of 'not being drawn in'. She maintains ongoing contact with the schools and invests in giving Asher the individual attention that he needs. In addition, she follows the structure of the daily routine outlined during the first weeks of counselling: preparing the home before bedtime for the next morning as well as following the new wake-up routines.

The mediator

The hardest assignment for Mrs Halpern is establishing a wider support network. Of necessity, this means exposing the family's problems to the outside world. With that she must overcome her pride in the face of her late husband's friends who have cut off contact since his death. One such person is a rabbi who holds a prominent position in the community. The team emphasizes to Mrs Halpern that without a support network the plan cannot materialize. Thus, she must gather the courage to face the father's friends. In the meantime, a list of immediate supporters is drawn up, including her sisters, her aunt and the avrekh who studies with the children.

In spite of the fact that she is showing signs of severe exhaustion, with the team's encouragement, she succeeds in overcoming the fear and shame barrier and turns to the rabbi who was a close friend of her late husband. Despite her hesitation and fear of rejection and much to her surprise, he responds positively to her. The team consequently contacts the rabbi and he agrees to come with her to the next session.

Mrs Halpern and the rabbi arrive to the fourth session. The team presents the rabbi with the rationale behind the model, stressing the importance of him mobilizing support for Mrs Halpern. For his part, the rabbi responds openly and positively and offers to shed light on the complex relations that the father's family has cultivated with Daniel. He confirms the fact that the father's family is sabotaging the mother's standing and inciting her son against her. Solidly identifying with the operative principles presented to him, the rabbi agrees to establish contact with Daniel and Jona to prepare them for the upcoming declaration, and promises to contemplate specific solutions to the plight of each child – work for Jona and a new school for Daniel.

In this meeting the declaration takes shape. As a close friend of the father, the rabbi will orchestrate the meeting. Playing the central role as a mediator acceptable to all sides, he will point to the family's weakness and to the violence that has ravaged the household. In addition, he will help the mother to assume her position as the head of the family. The brother who lives abroad will be notified and will join in the declaration event via a conference call. A list of seven supporters is drawn up, aside from the close friends of the father whom the rabbi will enlist. The declaration will be performed in the rabbi's synagogue. Thus, the act of restoring the family pyramid with the mother at the top and the children at the base is ready.

The declaration: a rite of passage

In the evening, the rabbi, Mrs Halpern, all ten of her children (the brother who lives abroad joins via conference call), her two sisters, six supporters/friends of the father, the social worker who worked with the mother, the avrekh and two members of the research team, get together in the synagogue. The rabbi opens the evening by saying that he feels a personal obligation to remind them of their father's legacy. As he derived most of his strength from his family, if the father could see what was going on in his family from his grave, he would be filled with pain. Following the rabbi, the mother rises to speak. Thanking all those who came, she tells them about how difficult her situation is and about her strong desire to bring an end to the violence and neglect in her home. She then invites the children to share their opinions.

Issac, the son who lives abroad, calls to pull down the barriers between the older and younger children, as well as to find ways to strengthen their sense of mutual co-operation and responsibility. Jona suggests a weekly family meeting that will provide an opportunity for family members to air their ideas, at the same time providing a reason for the family to get together. Shulem and Aaron each speak of the need to be more loving, to volunteer their time to help in the community, to continue to live and be joyful in spite of their loss and their difficult family situation.

Each supporter in turn gives an account of his personal experience, and then a unanimous suggestion arises collectively. Each is willing to serve as a personal mentor to one of the children, inviting him every second Sabbath, so as to lighten the mother's load.

All this time, Daniel sits quietly yet it is obvious that this meeting is hard on him. As one of the supporters addresses the group, he suddenly bursts into the talk to criticize his mother. The argument is deflected when one of the team members suggests that the issue that he raised will be carefully considered in the upcoming joint meeting between him and his mother, emphasizing the point of 'only if you want to do so'.

After the supporters, the avrekh takes his turn and the research team then closes the speaking part of the event. At the end of the declaration, there is a clear division of labour. The rabbi takes on the role of mediating between the mother and Daniel, as well as finding him a new school. Another supporter takes upon himself the task of finding work for Jona.

The increased community support has a noticeable impact on Mrs Halpern's motivation to act with restraint in the face of her children's difficult behaviour. The impressive declaration event brings to a head four weeks of the intervention. Intensive effort was invested in rehabilitating the mother's self-esteem and restoring her faith in her own abilities, in spite of the deep scarring left from the terrible past experiences. Her success in these objectives was clearly demonstrated in the way that she enlisted supporters, brought her family to the gathering, and stood tall while openly sharing the seriousness of what was going on in her home and the changes she planned to institute.

By the time the declaration event came to a close, the feeling that something truly great had occurred in this room was palpable. The declaration, and the remarkable way in which it was performed, certainly earned its qualification as a rite of passage.

TWO EXTRA MEETINGS

During the week after the declaration, two meetings that were not part of the formal intervention take place, each of them with serious implications for the family. Presumably, the lifting of the shroud of secrecy that hovered over the family's past and present during the declaration event is what enables these meetings to take place.

On his own initiative, Daniel asks to meet with his mother and asks that the research team and the rabbi be present. At this meeting, the rabbi takes the opportunity to speak to Daniel about his father's complex personality. A generous person who provided tremendous support for his community, he loved his family above all. However, in the same breath, the rabbi also mentions his stormy temperament and his objectionable and sometimes violent behaviour towards his wife. The rabbi suggests to Daniel that he adopt his father's former characteristics of warmth and generosity rather than the latter.

Before Daniel joins the meeting, a preparatory discussion is held with Mrs Halpern. This helps her to process her thoughts on the near-impossible role that her son has assumed. Representing his father in the family, Daniel feels it is his moral obligation to fight his father's unfinished battles with his mother. Consequently, the brothers reduce contact with him and Daniel becomes the outcast amongst them. Without a room of his own, he sleeps on a bed in the living room when he comes home for the weekends. Daniel seethes with anger and rage. With regard to the issue of his younger brothers, Daniel's eyes light up: 'If I can't play with them by hitting them, how else can I play with them?'

The mother is asked to help her son to complete the mourning process, by making the distinction between life and death. In order to enable him to connect to the good sides of his father, she is to convey to him that she does not, nor does any other family member, bear ill feelings towards his father. As for Daniel's claims that she hated his father and hated his whole appearance, the team helps the mother to articulate an answer which will confirm to Daniel that she very much wanted to continue to live together with his father and that she was very attracted by his appearance. Likewise, she loves her son's appearance, she is proud of his strong physique and she has no intention of subduing him. However, she would like to see him direct his capabilities in a way that benefits himself and his environment.

The atmosphere during the discussion is tense. Yet in spite of this and in spite of the fact that the mother has to leave temporarily when she cannot bear the harsh accusations and complaints that Daniel throws at her, she returns and rejoins the session. In this forum, mother and son succeed for the first time in a very long time, to have a relatively calm conversation on issues that really matter.

In response to Jona's request, an additional meeting is scheduled between the mother, the rabbi and Jona. According to the mother and the rabbi, the purpose of meeting is threefold: to encourage him to go out to work, to encourage him to be open to undergoing psychological treatment, and to encourage him to increase his level of participation and co-operation at home. Jona, however, has another agenda in mind. For his part, Jona takes advantage of this forum as a platform from which he announces a change in his lifestyle. He informs his mother and the rabbi in no uncertain terms that a life dictated by religious rules is not his life. On the one hand, he repeatedly swears of his love for his mother and his family. Yet, at the same time, he sees his development as separate from theirs. Even though such an announcement is heavy and dramatic, especially within the context of the community, still the forum proceeds calmly and uneventfully. Jona agrees that although he will be living a secular lifestyle himself, he will be careful not to do so in a way that compromises his mother or his family.

THE FOLLOW-UP: RECONCILIATION

In the shadow of the struggle that lies ahead with Daniel, Mrs Halpern comes to the final meeting. The team encourages her to reflect on the meeting with Daniel and acknowledge that he wants a real and equal place within the family, as one of the brothers. However, her substantial and impressive achievements of the recent past are undercut by her fear that Daniel's aberrant behaviour will impact on the younger children. She is also instructed to continue to engage in unconditional gestures of reconciliation towards him. The staff addresses the question of how she can engage in these acts in spite of his acts of outright hostility and provocation: how does she suggest dedicating special time for being together? How is she to find these time intervals before the provocation, before the hostility erupts and develops into full-scale confrontation? The place for gestures or reconciliation is over once the escalation process is in full swing.

During the meeting, the therapeutic staff highlights her major accomplishments: her move from passivity and powerlessness to action, her enlisting of supporters, her performance of sit-ins, getting the kids back to school, setting up each child in the school setting best suited to him. However, the achievement that outshines all others is her decision to take responsibility for her family. Although she has a great deal of work ahead of her, she must take the time to pause and be gratified by the intensive efforts that she has invested in the past six weeks. The staff strongly encourages her to continue to adhere to the operative principles of the Non-Violent Resistance Model.

SUMMARY OF THE INTERVENTION PROCESS: RETURNING THE PYRAMID TO ITS NATURAL STATE

There is no doubt that this case posed a serious therapeutic challenge for a number of reasons:

- the family's large size
- the family's troubled past
- many of its members carrying pathological symptoms
- the need to focus on one member while being open to the wider issue of the entire family
- the myriad problems engendered by violence and neglect.

Yet, in spite of all the difficulties, the mother's courageous response and the enthusiasm with which she mobilized into action made the change possible. The entire effort can be reduced to one critical objective: to restore the mother to her rightful position as head of the family. Although by the end of the intervention there are still many challenges in store for the family, the intervention has succeeded in moving them into the realm of the possible.

The core of this specific intervention lay in her shattering the taboo, lifting the shroud of secrecy that hovered over her home, opening the door and making a pact with those people on the outside who had some connection to the family. Reducing isolation is ultimately what empowered the mother to turn her kids around. In addition to effecting change, she also manages to mobilize her children as partners in the process. In this intensive, unrelenting process, the mother reveals that the 'boy-enemy' Daniel not only has one voice but that many voices speak within him, not only the voices of anger and violence, but also the voice that expresses his desire to relate, just like his brothers, to his mother. In her other son, Jona, she finds a voice that wants to make his own way without diminishing his love towards his family. In both of these encounters, the mother grows beyond her desire to change the child and stretches her ability to accept and to contain the difficulties to the limit. Overcoming the tough barrier of shame and blame, she regains her position at the helm of her family. She manages this in spite of her status as a widow in a very conservative community. Even though the religious community has its own language and ideas, the operative model with its principles and ideas are unequivocally accepted and adapted. The climax of the process occurs in the last meeting where Mrs Halpern informs the staff that she intends to go back to studying.

In spite of her remarkable progress, a host of unresolved issues remain that include financial dependence, self-esteem damaged by a radical change in quality of life and community standing, and a troubled relationship with Daniel.

EPILOGUE

Shortly after the meeting with the rabbi described above, without any definite plans and without having received any professional treatment, Jona leaves home and travels abroad. He settles there and finds a respectable job at a local bank. The rabbi finds Daniel a yeshiva abroad where he ultimately settles. Ultimately, Daniel establishes a civil relationship with his mother who travels abroad to visit him. With the help of the rabbi, the mother succeeds in finding resources to fund private counselling for Aaron, Shulem and David and for her continued professional guidance according to the principles of the Non-Violent Resistance Model.

CHAPTER NINE

The Child, the Parent and the School

The parent–child–school relationship is complex and exposes the deep impact a school can have on the behaviour of a troubled child.

This example differs from previously presented cases, as it was carried out in the setting of a private clinic and not as part of the research project. Features such as the telephone support conversation are carried out here when necessary, rather than being structured and formally scheduled as in the project. The presentation of this example will therefore differ slightly from those presented earlier.

The case concerns one of the most fundamental questions about parenting: how and to what extent does parental responsibility materialize itself when the situation with the child seems already desperate and all past and planned actions seem to be futile? Another important question which arises in this case concerns authority: how does the school interpret the responsibility, defined by law, towards the child?

Mrs Werner, a widow for seven years, is in her mid-forties, holds an academic job and has two children: Ron, 14 years old, and Zoe, 12 years old. She calls the clinic to set an urgent appointment for two reasons. Her son Ron displays violent behaviour at home, towards her and her daughter, and seems to be totally out of control. He is about to be expelled from school after staying at home for two months and refusing to go to school. With an urgent, almost terrified, tone, she explains that she needs immediate help.

To set the background to this case, it is important to describe the last incident with Ron that led Mrs Werner to ask for therapy. It gives a good idea of the state of affairs at the Werner's home – many similar incidents, always very intense, have become common experience. Mrs Werner describes how Ron phoned her at work demanding money for a new computer game. When she refused, Ron threatened to demolish the flat, cursed her with the worst possible language and hung up on her. On returning from work she found all her clothes thrown in the garden, many torn apart.

Zoe locked herself in her room until her mother arrived. While Mrs Werner rushed to her daughter's room, Ron's rage was re-inflamed, and the horrible incident came to a head with Ron running after the two with a knife in his hand, threatening to kill them both. The two escaped to the car, while Ron appeared on the terrace shouting and cursing. The family lives on the second floor of an apartment building in a well-to-do area. In spite of the dramatic shouting, no one seems to have taken any notice of the incident. The two wander around the city, waiting to be able to go back home, hoping that Ron has calmed down after his harsh outburst of the afternoon. Four hours later they return to find Ron sitting quietly at his PC making threatening faces at them.

BACKGROUND: A TROUBLED HOME

Mrs and the late Mr Werner, who originated from Portugal and Spain respectively, settled in Portugal where they had Ron and Zoe. Mrs Werner, who was an established scientist, went to work and Mr Werner stayed at home, taking care of the kids and waiting for a breakthrough as a writer. Around the time Ron was five years old the family decided to immigrate to Germany, where again, Mrs Werner went to work and Mr Werner stayed at home.

Mrs Werner describes her late husband as a person of colourful character, lovable and loving to his kids. However, the long years of waiting in vain for success to come turned him into a desperate and depressed individual, sometimes acting out of rage. Nevertheless, the two children were strongly attached to him, especially Ron.

Ron is eight years old and Zoe is six, when their father is found dead in his bed early one morning. From then on, between coming back from school and Mrs Werner's return from work at seven in the evening, the children are looked after by different adults and young babysitters.

The home

The first impression at the Werner's front door is that of noise and chaos. Overwhelming loud rock music is mixed with the sound of a computer war game, barking dogs and screaming birds. The living room is where most of this is happening. Ron is usually seated next to the PC that operates at maximum volume, surrounded by three to five friends who will habitually remain until the middle of the night, moving around and using the room and the kitchen as they please. Ron and his friends make fun of Zoe when she dares to cross the living room to come to the kitchen. Most of the time she will stay locked in her room, waiting for her mother to come home from work. Ron and his friends ignore Mrs Werner's presence as well as her requests to turn the PC's volume and the music down. It is common for Ron to tell his friends 'Just ignore the stupid cow.'

Ron's relationship with his mother and sister fluctuates between short-lived gestures of interest and displays of affection, frequent un-expected verbal and dramatic physical displays of rage, loss of control and bullying the sister in the mother's presence and absence. Zoe's complaints of being afraid to sleep alone in her room are becoming more frequent and intense. She complains of severe migraines that often prevent her from attending school. She is quite isolated in the school playground and displays difficulties in coping both academically and socially with her classmates. She is in constant need of as-sistance with her school assignments. As soon as Mrs Werner arrives home from work, both withdraw to Mrs Werner's room where they do home work and watch TV together. Although Mrs Werner complains that she is tired of providing the constant help that Zoe requires, she describes her as an affectionate child and admits to seeing her as an ally who helps her through the troubled times at home. Obviously, Ron perceives it as rejection, directed against him especially since all his attempts to be at ease and communicate with his sister are turned down. It seems that Ron is unaware of his abusive behaviour and the fact that his sister and mother are afraid of him.

Any attempt by Mrs Werner or Zoe to reclaim the use of the living room is met by Ron with heavy verbal abuse in front of his friends who remain indifferent to Mrs Werner's demands for them to leave her house. Normally, Ron will tell them: 'ignore this witch, she is simply crazy'. When the friends leave, Ron goes to his mother's room, no matter how late it is, and threatens to demolish the flat if she dares embarrass him again in front of his friends. The threats are usually accompanied by extremely abusive words. When Ron eventually calms down he falls asleep in the living room with all the lights on. If undisturbed by his mother, he will sleep until late afternoon and only wake up when his friends are about to visit again. Often Ron pretends to be ready to go to school and sneaks back to bed after Mrs Werner leaves for work.

At school

Both Ron and Zoe are diagnosed with attention deficit hyperactivity disorder (ADHD) with social problems. While Ron prefers contact with older peers at school who play the role of outsiders themselves, Zoe is extremely isolated at school. Up to the point where the intervention begins, their father's death is kept a secret from friends and even teachers. And although the fact is documented at the school, it seems totally forgotten by all involved. The school is not informed about the situation at home.

Ron stops attending school and his academic achievements are so poor that his teachers cannot even write a general evaluation regarding his performance. Nonetheless the school demands Ron's regular attendance and full participation in classes, exams and social activities. A general complaint from all teachers is that Ron seldom responds when addressed and when asked to answer he refuses to do so. The teachers consider him to be disrespectful and extremely arrogant. A representative of the Ministry of Education made one home visit, but it had no consequences. Mrs Werner complains that the school treats her and Ron indifferently and feels a deep sense of alienation. Any contact with the school leaves her deeply hurt and humiliated.

Based on Mrs Werner's report, the following is a list of reasons for Ron's violent outbursts:

1. Waking him up in the morning.

2. Dismissing complaints about dizziness, stomach pain and excessive sweating which the mother dismisses as make-believe.

3. The mother insisting that Ron goes to school in spite of the above complaints.

4. Denying one of his demands, be it money or ad hoc demands to be driven to school (Ron refuses to use public transport services).

5. Insisting that Ron should allow Zoe to use the PC for her school assignments.

6. Demanding that his friends do not come every day and at least leave before midnight when they do.

7. Retreating behind closed doors – each time Mrs Werner and her daughter retreat to her bedroom.

THERAPY STEPS

It is easy to establish a list of possible causes for Ron's violent behaviour: the loss of a father figure, his mother's physical absence (she spends long hours at work) and mental absence (overtired, impatient and distracted), losing control when confronted with Ron's disobedience and disrespect, cursing him and telling him he would end up in the streets as an idiot.

Special attention is directed in the initial stages of the therapy at explaining how her withdrawal, together with her daughter to her room, is most probably perceived by Ron as a hostile act. Mrs Werner is incapable of showing any enthusiasm about things he considers 'cool' or interesting. Ron has taught himself to play the electric guitar and masters complicated PC programs for processing pictures, animations, and websites. Though Mrs Werner realizes how valuable such accomplishments are, she is not able to bring herself to praise him for it, or even just sit and listen to the music he plays, nor is she interested in seeing what he produces on the PC. She states: 'I cannot bring myself to show him any affection. I simply cannot anymore. I feel burnt out.'

Mrs Werner gives an authentic account of her lifestyle, of how overworked she is at her job and at home, of having no social or cultural life and of feeling desperate and depressed about the kids' prospects. She entertains very limited contact with a few relatives from her late husband's side. She is ashamed to invite people to her home and gave up completely on the idea of romance or a relationship with a new partner.

Mrs Werner is coached according to the principles of the Non-Violent Resistance Model. She is asked to contemplate her habitual actions and reactions towards Ron, and how she may possibly fuel his aggression by being absent and dismissive. Special emphasis is given to introducing her to ideas about the nature and characteristics of aggressive behaviour and how oscillating between capitulation and violent outburst intensify escalation and reproduce ever harsher exchanges. Special attention is given to the idea that physical withdrawal and detachment are one and the same, namely just another form of aggression. Mrs Werner is introduced to the idea of the possible strong link between anxiety, depression and aggression, all threads that characterize the behaviour of the three of them: Ron, Zoe and herself.

Soon it becomes apparent that the primary goal of the intervention needs to focus first and foremost on the attempt to restrain Ron's violent behaviour at home while the problems at school must wait. The principles of the Non-Violent Resistance Model are presented to Mrs Werner as the tools for accomplishing de-escalation of the violent exchanges with Ron together with establishing a normal dialogue and rapport with him. Mrs Werner is sent home with instructions to create a list of possible supporters who will accompany her in the process and attend the event where the declaration and sit-in should take place. The supporters should provide Mrs Werner with support and enable the event to be carried out without violent outbursts. Meanwhile, Mrs Werner is advised to abstain from any violent or aggressive action or remark on her part. Zoe is also instructed to try to be responsive when Ron seeks her company. It is decided to hold the next session as soon as Mrs Werner comes up with the supporter list. Naturally, to request the help of the supporters she has in mind, Mrs Werner will have to get over her reluctance and strong sense of shame and embarrassment in revealing the ongoing violence at home. It is also agreed that for the time being, Mrs Werner will contact the therapist when the situation dictates a need for help. However, Mrs Werner has a problem with what seems to be obvious and inevitable: that in order to recruit help, the long kept secret of the troubled home life will have to be made public. It takes her four weeks to prepare the list of supporters.

The sit-in and the declaration event take place in the Werners' living room together with a couple of friends, her boss and his wife, a neighbour and the therapist. The only person known to the children is the neighbour. When all are gathered, Mrs Werner asks Ron to join the group as she has an important announcement to make. To her astonishment Ron joins without opposition, and sits quietly listening to his mother's introduction of the group that begins by saying that these people came upon her invitation since she no longer knows how to handle the situation at home. The therapist takes it from there and begins with the statement that the gathering is an act intended to help him, his sister and his mother to denounce the violent behaviour that seems to dominate all exchanges at the Werners' home. He says that the decision has been made to help them take an active stand against it and that violence is clearly intolerable and unacceptable. All participants in this meeting are determined to provide Mrs Werner, Ron and his sister with the necessary help in order to take this stand. Thereafter, the mother reads a well-prepared declaration, which was formulated in the spirit of the Non-Violent Resistance principles. Each of the people present at the meeting adds their commitment to help the family confront the violence. Astonishingly, Ron sits quietly and seems to be totally concentrated, listening to the detailed description of his behaviour and the situation at home, to his mother's declaration and to the encouragement of the others. When encouraged to react especially to his mother's words, he promises to exercise control over his verbal and physical rage. Zoe adds her statement that she will no longer be ready to tolerate being bullied by Ron and declares her commitment to do all that is required of her to begin to mend the relationship at home. One of the attendees promises to establish regular contact with Ron (which materializes as a steady and solid contact for years to come). Calling cards and private mobile phone numbers of all the participants are given to both children. They are encouraged to make a call for help or advice whenever they need it without hesitation.

Two days later the therapist receives a phone call from Ron, asking for a meeting with the condition that his mother and his sister should come as well. For the following two months the three of them appear for a weekly session. The main topic is the violent behaviour as a form of stress. In addition, the new order in the family hierarchy is negotiated. During these two months Ron reveals a cascade of complaints.

He believes that the entire world is against him, that the school and especially his mother do not understand him or protect his well-being. They do not have an interest in him as a person or his needs and nobody shows any interest in the things he values. His mother offends him and humiliates him regularly and prefers his sister.

A new diagnosis is formulated for Ron: severe depression accompanied with anxiety attacks and manifestations of rage and aggression as well as agoraphobia which leads to school truancy.

This period of the intervention concentrates on encouraging the mother to set clear basic boundaries and enhancing her awareness of Ron's complaints by helping her to differentiate between legitimate and unreasonable complaints. These deliberations are accompanied with a constant and careful effort to prevent words and conduct that might fuel harsh reaction and escalation in the family. During this period Ron reveals other facets of his personality: a great sense of humour, rich fantasy, compassion with animals (he often brings a dog to the session), enthusiasm about his music and PC design – all attributes that his mother seems to disregard or not to recognize in her son. The sessions offer a good opportunity for Ron to demonstrate them. The hard mutual accusations are slowly replaced by understanding the other's point of view. This is accompanied by good humour at each other's own failure and the situation.

The noticeable change that appears is an ongoing improvement of the atmosphere at the Werners' home. Manifestations of rage and escalation become few and far between. The family begins to enjoy spending time together, free of harsh exchanges and disputes. However, Ron is still at home having immense difficulty restoring a normal daily routine, complaining of dizziness, sweating and pain in the stomach and heart. The idea of getting back to school creates total panic. On the other hand, the bond between Ron and the therapist is growing steadily and in spite of his anxiety he is open to working with her on an individual basis. The target is now getting Ron back to school.

BACK TO SCHOOL

As described at the beginning, the school seems to have given up on Ron and apart from polite enquiry about his absence now and again, there has been no apparent effort to help or provide a solution except for the last threat to expel him from school.

At this stage, the mother is asked to initiate contact with Ron's school. A meeting with his class teacher and the school counsellor is set and the therapist also attends it. The idea is to mobilize both of them to work out a plan that encourages Ron's return to school. Since the mother is completely reluctant to reveal the situation at home in front of the two, it is decided not to go into the subject but rather to stress that it is growing out of control for Mrs Werner, and that she badly needs the school's help and co-operation. Already, at the beginning of the meeting, the class teacher appears reluctant to consider any suggestions that deviate from her routine. She remains indifferent to the description of Ron's psychological state and keeps repeating how short she is with time and that regular visits to school as well as keeping up with the requested level of achievements are trivial and mandatory demands. She stresses her commitment to those demands, saying she does not see how she can bend them for Ron's sake. The background and reasons that were introduced by the therapist seem to make no difference to her point of view. She keeps saying: 'Ron needs to behave like the others.' However, the school counsellor seems to be more receptive and signals her readiness to become more actively involved to establish personal contact with Ron and advocate a special programme for him. A new meeting is scheduled with her to elaborate on the programme presented by the therapist. Mrs Werner leaves the meeting extremely hurt and disappointed by the teacher's response. It takes quite an effort to convince her that in spite of everything, the meeting was successful as the school counsellor has become an ally. However the therapist stresses that Mrs Werner had to go one step further – to speak openly about the problems at home.

At the second meeting, the mother describes Ron's history while the therapist establishes the link between depression, anxiety and violence in Ron's behaviour and how they lead to agoraphobia and truancy. It is agreed to start behavioural training with Ron in order to enable him to overcome the anxiety and get back to school. The school counsellor agrees to be an active partner in executing the following measures:

1. She visits Ron's home, to express her support and willingness to work hand in hand with the plan presented by the therapist.

2. Ron is driven to school three times with the therapist, each time approaching the school a little more. The school counsellor waits for him at the gate to greet him and walks all the way to the car to do so. Eventually, on the third occasion, Ron dares to step out of the car and walk to the gate. He also accepts the idea of trying to enter the school and go to the counsellor's office. On the following day, the counsellor waits for Ron at the school gate and leads him together with the therapist to her office. She suggests that he comes to her office to help her organize her PC and work with her on some important presentations she has to carry out. Ron accepts the offer and the therapist leaves the two to plan their work. From then on Ron comes every morning to work with the counsellor as agreed. She not only establishes a routine for Ron to come to school daily, but also helps him to renew contact with class and schoolmates. She encourages them to wait for Ron in front of her office, inviting them in to take interest in the work she and Ron do together. On their part they keep inviting Ron to spend breaks with them at the schoolyard. It becomes a welcomed routine for Ron. His bond with the counsellor becomes solid and she is growing enthusiastic about the plan and Ron's progress. Ron is sure that she is genuinely fond of him. Slowly but surely, Ron expands his territory at school and often reacts more positively to spontaneous invitations from peers to join them at the schoolyard.

3. At this stage Ron is introduced to the person in charge of the PC system and programming at school. It is the second male with whom Ron establishes a warm relationship during this process. The affinity here is based on the enthusiasm to share knowledge about PCs and a more important aspect: the PC administrator originates from the same country Ron's late father came from. The laboratory is located in the same building where Ron's class is situated, a building that in spite of all the progress, Ron has avoided until now. It is decided to acknowledge Ron's performance with the PC administrator like any other academic achievement. This part of the plan is working wonderfully – Ron is working with him on the

design of the school web page and Ron comes to school with enthusiasm and readiness that astonishes everyone. Ron is now ready to discuss getting back to class.

4. At the next big school conference, the counsellor invites the therapist to present Ron's case in front of the school director and the general teaching assembly. It is an act that finally legitimizes the plan which was so carefully orchestrated. At the end of the meeting it is agreed that Ron will go back to his regular class and attend maths, English and French lessons as well as the weekly general hour carried out by the class teacher. From now on Ron visits these lessons regularly and the rest of the time he spends in the computer lab.

5. Based on the therapist's report the counsellor organizes home tutoring and though Ron is not enthusiastic about it, he copes well with the young teacher.

Fundamental to the process, and therefore emphasized here again, is the warm relationship Ron establishes with the counsellor and the PC administrator. As agreed with them, they make the effort to enquire about Ron even if he is not scheduled to see them. This personal contact turns to be the solid base on which Ron is finally able to operate and exhibit good achievements within the agreed framework. Ron continues to develop his musical skills and to demonstrate highly creative skills. At this stage we witness completely peaceful conduct at home. All signs of violence retreat and the work with Ron and his family concentrates on improving the sibling relationship and tackling the chaos that governs their home.

TRANSITION

This balanced and positive status quo lasts for two years. However, the balance is shaken once Ron enters the eleventh grade. With the transition, all main figures in Ron's newly agreed school routine change: the class teacher, school counsellor and school director. Already with the first telephone call, the new counsellor expresses scepticism regarding whether the old agreement with Ron will continue to be carried out. She states right away that she is very preoccupied and that she will probably not be able to be as engaged as her former colleague. It is evident that a different agenda is on the table. The school aspires for successful students to perform well for the matriculation certificate. Ron disturbs the nice statistics success that the school prefers to present.

At the following meeting, the school director, the new school counsellor, the former one, Mrs Werner, Ron and the therapist meet to discuss the situation. The school director conducts the meeting in a high-handed manner leaving little room for the counsellor to speak. Ignoring Mrs Werner and Ron, he directs his speech to the therapist stating how he appreciates Ron's needs and acknowledges the progress that he has made, but concluding that Ron needs a suitable school to meet his special needs. He declares that the school's main target is clearly to prepare the students to excel in their matriculation exams, and though Ron's case requires special consideration, his attitude towards Ron and similar students is: 'not in my school'. While Ron and his mother sink into total silence, the former counsellor seems extremely uncomfortable listening to her colleague echoing the school director's position. The presentation of why it would be best for Ron to graduate with his peers in the school that he finally grew attached to awakes no resonance. For Ron it is a harsh decision, since the schools that are offered as adequate are not at all suitable for him. It is a well-known fact that schools for students with special needs have students who often exhibit severe behavioural problems at school.

Summing up the options available to Ron, the therapist finds the decision very unfortunate and expresses her disappointment about failing to convince the school about the plan that seemed to work to Ron's benefit. She therefore encourages Mrs Werner to take the case to the Ministry of Education. Soon afterwards, the Ministry of Education accepts the therapist's recommendation and Ron remains at school in spite of the school policy and its director's objection.

From then on Ron continues to go to school, fulfilling an extensive programme, newly tailored for him, with the aim of partially reaching the demands for his matriculation. However, contact with his class teacher is substantially reduced and though the school counsellor makes certain efforts to meet him regularly, the contact soon becomes destabilized. The old sense of not being seen and appreciated reappears. Staying at home, complaining about dizziness, head and stomach aches, become more and more frequent. The stress at home begins to take its toll on Ron and his family.

Ron's case demonstrates certain aspects that we consider to be of great importance:

- It is pointless to raise, even discuss, the subject of achievements before we eliminate violence and destructive behaviour.

- Eliminating violence and restricting destructive behaviour is the first essential elementary action in the process of healing.

- It is imperative for all participants to act together. It is never a case for isolated effort.

SUMMARY

In Ron's case we have seen that immediately after the first measure was incorporated – the sit-in event – the harsh violent exchanges ceased and Ron was seen to be a young, anxious and depressed individual, eager to be heard and seen, rather than just a violent boy. Only then could an effort be made to help him reclaim his natural and healthy performance. Personal contact played a crucial role in Ron's well-being. More specifically, the case clearly demonstrates how his personal contact with his guidance counsellor at school inspired him to demonstrate his abilities, talent and achievements. Personal contact is the prerequisite to all good performance. School can be a frightening and alienating experience, especially for children like Ron, with such a troubled history. The personal contact, as exercised for the first two years with the school counsellor and the PC specialist, made the whole difference for Ron.

The case raises the cardinal question about the values of the school system. The first school counsellor demonstrated a willingness to adapt to the ideas of the Non-Violent Resistance Model that were presented to her. She was eager to view Ron and his background as one, ready to work hand in hand with the therapist and showed compassion towards Ron and his mother. It was a completely new experience for Ron and Mrs Werner. With time, the counsellor convinced all the teachers responsible for Ron at school with her enthusiasm. She became the best advocate of the idea that Ron's success depended among other things on the co-operation of all participants – that only with a joint effort and with them all utilizing the same language and the same values could Ron recover. She recruited the support of the pedagogic committee, using the therapist's expertise to present the case and the working model. On this level of operation, the interpretation of the Non-Violent Resistance Model produced outstanding results that impacted on Ron's life at school and at home beyond all expectations. With the move to the eleventh grade, we found that the school's main priority was to demonstrate its high standards through the high scores of its students. At this level there was no more room for personal involvement and commitment between the educators and the students. Quite the opposite, the interpretation of the Non-Violent Resistance Model in school life is based on the readiness to:

1. maintain personal contact with the student

2. move away from conventional and normative solutions and sanctions

3. create a transparent process in which all participants on all levels of the hierarchy at school are aware and are well informed about the measures taken

4. adapt the model's language as a normative language for the whole school system.

If we dare to take one more step forward we could say that it is essential to restructure the value system dominating schools today. With such a renewed set of values, the school should aspire to be the place where students first and foremost feel secure, since only under such conditions can achievements, knowledge and the growth of personality flourish. This is a political statement that leads us back to the beginning of the ideas presented in this book and to Gandhi and all other sources upon which the working model of Non-Violent Resistance is based.

CHAPTER TEN

The Model of Non-Violent Resistance: A Guidebook for Parents

The phenomenon of children or adolescents, whose patterns of behaviour are typically disruptive poses a tough challenge for parents and professionals alike. An increased tendency to argue, a lack of boundaries, anger and threats, are all part of the long list of characteristics which tend to be used to describe such children. Common to all these behaviours is the uncompromising stand – 'I am the boss!' This statement encapsulates the defining characteristic of the defiant, non-compliant child.

Parents soon learn that their repertoire of coping methods, including suggestions given to them by professionals, is not sufficient to satisfactorily deal with the problem. Their experience shows that their admonitions, yells, threats and punishments perpetuates, at times even worsens, their child's behaviour. On the other hand, appeasing him only serves to increase his demands. Under such conditions, the home meant to serve as a haven becomes a battlefield with parents and their children perennially engaged. The potential for escalation lurks within

Note: The *Guidebook for Parents* appeared for the first time in Omer, Weinblatt and Avraham-Krehwinkel (2002). A German edition was prepared by Avraham-Krehwinkel in 2001. This current *Guidebook* – a revised and expanded version that has been written in the English language – is the work of Avraham-Krehwinkel.

each fragmentary argument and divisive encounter. In this situation, war-weary parents often find themselves on the verge of exhaustion, ready to retreat.

It is no wonder then that some parents, aching for a little peace and quiet, find themselves ready to declare their defeat. Yet experience proves that the relief that comes through surrender is all too brief. It is quickly followed by increased demands from the child. This self-nourishing process adds its own momentum and strength, leaving the parents feeling as if they have come to a dead end. They have become unwilling partners in the cycle of:

Surrender → increased demands on the part of the child → parents' hostility towards him → increased hostility on his part, and so on.

In this cycle, escalation dictates almost all courses of action – the parents' and the child's.

It is possible to distinguish between two types of escalation:

- **Escalation of hostility**: hostility that breeds further hostility.

- **Escalation of demands**: as parents submit the child steps up his demands and his aggression.

When the child escalates his behaviour, that is when the child begins to threaten, scream, go wild or becomes physically aggressive when his demands are not met, parents either acquiesce or try to forcibly impose their authority. Unfortunately, this response encourages the child to become more extreme. A different type of escalation is asymmetrical. It is expressed when the parent gives in, transmitting a weak image to the child – that they are unable to manage the child's or their own outbursts. The child then gains confidence in using threats or violence to get his way. These two types of escalation feed on each other – the more the parents yield, the more they become angry, frustrated and prone to outbursts. Yet, as the mutual outbursts become more severe, they also become ever more frightening, pushing the parents to the point where they feel ready to surrender. In this atmosphere of on-going, intensifying escalation, it is no wonder that parents feel less and less able to express or sense their love for their child.

NON-VIOLENT RESISTANCE

Non-Violent Resistance is a tool which enables parents to block their child's destructive behaviour without inviting escalation, helping ultimately to create an atmosphere at home conducive to the expression of love and affection. Non-Violent Resistance is defined as a series of actions that impart the parent's message to the child, saying, 'I am not willing to continue living like this and I will do everything short of attacking you verbally or physically, to stop this situation.'

Non-Violent Resistance is characterized by the following principles:

1. Insisting with determination upon demands deemed right and important.

2. Attempting vigorously to obstruct the child's destructive behaviours.

3. Avoiding categorically any use of physically or verbally aggressive behaviour, such as hitting, cursing, blaming, threatening or humiliating the child.

Non-Violent Resistance affords parents a moral and practical basis for demonstrating parental presence and for monitoring their child's activities, enabling parents to minimize and ultimately prevent escalation.

Based on the notion that solid parental presence is the cornerstone of good relations between parent and child, the purpose of Non-Violent Resistance is to restore parental presence. As parents, the authority you are striving to achieve cannot be based on your being physically stronger than your child. It can only be based on your deep resolve to be with him and beside him. As you enhance your parental presence, the probability will rise that your child will eschew escalating patterns in favour of dialogue, as the basis of your mutual relationship.

THE 'PAUSE AND POSTPONE' PRINCIPLE AND THE PRINCIPLE OF 'NOT BEING DRAWN IN'

In order to avoid escalation and in order to construct a new relationship free of endless power struggles, you must avoid entering into conflict with your child. Your child, whose control is fed by threats and violence, will continually invite you into confrontation hoping thereby to gain the upper hand. There is a simple reason for all of this:

the aggressive child 'gains' by conflict, even when he does not come out 'on top'. It is enough that he has rattled you or made you lose control, to justify continuing his extreme behaviour. This pattern does not stem from his being 'bad' or 'mentally disturbed', but from having developed patterns of escalation – when the child does not get his way he simply escalates his behaviour.

You too, in all probability, have your own patterns of escalation. You too may have a 'short fuse' that prevents you from staying calm during disputes, causing you to lose control. Parents who cannot abstain from getting involved in confrontations with their children are typically verbose, preachy, and argumentative, using threats and shouting when dealing with their child. All these forms of parental verbiage and argumentative behaviour testify to the parent's inability to abstain from involvement, ultimately leading to escalation.

The following is a typical dialogue:

'You are not going!'

'Yes I am!'

'I said – you're not going!'

'You can't tell me what to do!'

'So long as you live in this house you will follow the house rules!'

'I don't have to ask you!' *(slamming the door)*

At the end, the child does what he wants, leaving you angry and exhausted. Escalation has occurred.

Many times, your attempts to explain things to, convince, preach to, and argue with your child, lead him only to further disregard or ignore you. Thus, the more you talk, the more helpless you feel.

Remember: Over-speaking is escalatory – it comes from helplessness. A clear restriction is infinitely better than explaining, preaching or trying to convince.

Threats such as 'If...then...!' will lead the child to threaten you in return.

The principle of 'not being drawn in' is accompanied by the 'pause and postpone' principle. Parents typically think, 'I must immediately respond to my child's every statement, complaint or provocation.' This is fundamentally wrong – you need not respond to everything. Instead you must practise delaying or postponing your response.

Therefore: take time in planning your response.

When in doubt, stay silent, rather than responding immediately.

Maintaining silence is time given, so your child can 'waste his ammunition'.

Remember: silence is not surrender.

If you wish, you may precede your silence with a few choice words, such as 'I do not like this, and I am going to think about it.' You must say it without any hint of a threat, merely as a matter of fact. After you repeat this a number of times, your child will come to understand that your silence is not the end of the matter. Silence without surrender is more powerful than preaching or arguing. You may think that your silence will be interpreted as a sign of weakness, to be taken advantage of by your child. On the contrary, silence announces your unwillingness to accept his invitations to confrontation, your desire for new avenues of communication without resorting to sermons or force.

It is important to emphasize that constructive silence is not detachment. Parental presence is not compromised by silence; on the contrary – it is enhanced by it. You are proving to yourself and to your child that you have the strength not to be drawn into conflicts – you are positioning yourselves independently as parents. These principles guide you when seeking to defuse episodes of escalation between you and your child.

Repeat to yourself silently when pressed: 'I will not be drawn into conflict, I will not be drawn into conflict, I will not be drawn into conflict!'

The emotional posture expressed through the dual principles of 'not being drawn in' and 'pause and postpone' is 'absorption'. Absorption allows your child's attacks to naturally dissolve. The posture of absorption addresses the two difficult emotions that invite surrender or escalation: frustration and rage. Frustration is the emotion which brings the parent to raise his hands in surrender, preferring to 'buy peace and quiet' through acquiescence. Rage is the emotion which brings the parent to try to get back at his child, using the child's own devices. Absorption allows the parent to maintain Non-Violent Resistance while avoiding both escalation and surrender. Putting both of those principles to use is the key for the success of the process called the 'sit-in' that follows the 'declaration'.

DECLARATION: THE STATEMENT OF INTENT

The declaration aims to voice the parents' position, their intention and their future moves. The central component is a statement regarding the parents' intention that all future action will be taken with transparency. This action also includes an appeal to all possible sources of future support. From this point of view, the declaration is seen as the turning point in the lives of those who are concerned with the process. You have now made a commitment – to yourselves, to your child, to your partner and to the process itself.

It is recommended that you inform your child, in advance, of your unequivocal decision to end your loneliness by sharing the situation with those around you. Informing your child in advance may prevent him from feeling that you have acted behind his back, and that you have 'turned him in' or 'betrayed' him. Knowing you have done all you can to inform him about your plans, enables you to meet such accusations, and affords you some sense of moral fortitude in continuing your struggle.

Informing your child should be done in a simple and practical manner, using no intimidation. It is recommended that you inform your child in writing, in addition to doing so verbally.

Drafting and timing your declaration

Pick a convenient time – long after a violent outburst – and announce your declaration in a calm, resolute, non-intimidating tone of voice.

As a parent, you have never taken a stand against your child's behaviour. You are now ready to declare your intentions, and take some time to reflect on your changed position. In your actions you send out a message that the die has been cast, that you now stand resolved and united.

Should you fear a violent reaction from your child, consider having a third party present. The presence of others significantly reduces, and most of the time even eliminates, the occurrence of violence.

If you cannot communicate directly with your child, ask a mediator to bring your written declaration to the child. Declarations should always be made orally and in writing. Even when you have already made your announcement orally and your child has heard you speak, the written word adds fortitude, empowering both word and action.

The content of the declaration

Recall one or two examples of your child's extreme behaviour in the past. Present these examples to your child, in order to emphasize how intolerable is the situation in which your family now finds itself. Attempt, as far as possible, to include a descriptive, rather than judgmental, message in your declaration. For example, instead of saying, 'We will no longer suffer the terror you have wrought in our household' say: 'We will no longer tolerate you beating up your brother and sister.'

Example of a draft declaration

The violence in our household has become intolerable. (*Here should follow a list of concrete negative behaviours.*) We cannot, and do not wish to, live like this anymore. We intend to do all that we can to change this situation, outside of attacking you verbally or physically.

Therefore:

- We have decided to become more present in your life.

- We have decided to no longer face these problems alone. We will seek out and turn to our friends and relatives, asking for their full involvement.

- We have decided to resolutely oppose the following behaviour. (*Here, cite one or two, but not more than three, specific examples of his extreme behaviour in the past.*)

- We do not want to overpower you, nor do we wish to defeat you.

- This statement bears no threat to you. It simply expresses our commitment to you, as your parents and as human beings.

The child's response to the declaration

The likelihood is that your child will resent the declaration. His reaction may be accompanied by direct escalation or by belittling, derisive words and actions. The child will follow familiar response patterns hoping to reap the familiar reactions. You must meet these escalatory expressions with resolved calm. Your quiet response, your choosing not to be drawn by your child's direct or implied invitation for escalation, will form the way you interact with your child from now on.

Should extreme behaviour reoccur following the declaration, ask those you have informed of the situation to contact the child personally or by telephone, mail, email or fax to tell your child that they have been fully informed regarding his behaviour. Ask them to refer specifically to the latest occurrence. They must make it clear to the child that they regard such behaviour as completely unacceptable. If he has been violent towards you or towards other family members, or if he has destroyed property, they must let him know that this type of behaviour constitutes 'violence within the family' and is considered a violation of the law. In general, they must impart to him their resolve to help you stop the situation, and their intention to fully support you. It is advisable that friends and family members be given this guidebook, so that they can familiarize themselves with the strategies and principles associated with the Non-Violent Resistance Model.

The purpose of communication between your supporters and your child is to clarify to your child that he can no longer hide his deeds, that his behaviour is catching outside attention and that those who know of it stand firmly behind you, while at the same time they intend to support him.

> **Remember: writing, as a means of communication, has its own unique power.**

Telephone calls, faxes and letters from far-away friends or relatives, whom the child holds in high regard, are especially effective.

> **Remember: all these steps make it known to your child that you are no longer alone.**

In many instances, the mere knowledge that you are not alone itself suffices in discernibly diminishing his extreme behaviour. Recruiting outside help is not an easy decision. You must overcome your inhibitions in carrying it through. However, once you have crossed that hurdle, and you have gathered sufficient inner strength to proceed, you will be fortified by the support of the people around you, and you will find that your child responds positively to your newfound support.

Consequently, your self-confidence will increase as well as your trust in the path that you have chosen.

Inviting outsiders may open up new avenues towards solutions. Beyond supporting you and serving as channels of moral persuasion (by representing public opinion), your supporters may potentially act as mediators. Among your friends or family members, you may find a person who is capable of communicating with the child, possibly working out compromises with him. These compromises could simply not be reached without mediation, as (a) both parties – you and your child – suffer from a lack of communication and (b) the child feels that he must hold on to his position to maintain his dignity. The mediator may also help persuade your child to back off from extreme positions in situations where your appeals would be automatically rejected (for example, persuading the child to come back home). The mediator greatly helps to minimize the loneliness children often feel under the new set of circumstances. It is in times of crisis – a child shutting himself in, or demonstrably leaving home – that mediators are most welcome. By simply involving the mediator, you have acted to reduce escalation and polarization.

The following sections will discuss another group of people that are capable of acting as mediators – your child's friends and their parents.

From the declaration – the statement of intent – we move on to action – to the tools employed by Non-Violent Resistance to achieve its goals.

THE SIT-IN

One of the most potent activities parents can engage in when practising Non-Violent Resistance is the 'sit-in'. The sit-in follows an extreme incident, allowing parents to demonstrate their presence while abstaining from confrontation.

A quiet sit-in demonstrates parental presence and expresses parental resolve. Its purpose is to make it known to your child that you stand resolved – that you will no longer tolerate your child's aggression.

How does the sit-in work?

1. Enter your child's room when he is there, at a time that is convenient for you. Do not do this immediately after an

extreme occurrence in the house. Do the sit-in some time later, at least a day later when you are calm and when you have blocked off a sufficient amount of time. Do not execute the sit-in when you are stressed for time – you must not leave in the middle.

2. Close the door to the room behind you and sit yourself down – on a chair, on the floor, on the carpet – in some way that makes it difficult for your child to leave the room.

3. Only once sitting, tell your child calmly: 'We will no longer tolerate your behaviour. (*Proceed to describe the behaviour you object to, citing specific examples.*) We have come here to find a way to solve this problem. We would like to hear your suggestions.'

4. Then sit quietly and await your child's suggestions.

5. Listen to what he has to say, and consider his words.

6. If they are accusations ('It is my brother's fault!'), demands ('Buy me a television set and I'll stop!'), or threats ('OK I'm going to run away!'), do not take the bait. Avoid confrontation! Tell him what he says is unacceptable, and continue to sit quietly. Avoid blames, threats, sermons or arguments of any kind. Keep waiting quietly and patiently. Under no circumstances allow yourself to be led into a verbal or physical confrontation. Time and silence project parental resolve.

7. Should the child make even the slightest positive suggestion, ask him to explain it.

8. Then, leave the room quietly, telling him positively that you will give it a chance. Do not threaten your child by saying that should he renege, you will come and sit in his room again. If the child repeats a suggestion that he has made in the past, tell him: 'You have already made that suggestion and it did not help. We now need something that will work better.'

9. If the child has not made any suggestion, remain in his room for up to one hour, then walk out. Do not warn or threaten that you will return. When leaving, you may simply say: 'We have not yet found a solution.'

Key points to remember

1. The sit-in must be planned in advance by the parents.

2. Undesirable behaviour must be clearly defined. Avoid using general messages, like 'We would like you to behave better.' Be specific: 'We want you to stop using foul language and to stop using hand gestures.'

3. Parents who expect their child to become violent should invite an adult to the house (a friend or close family member) but not into the room with them. Following the opening words, tell your child: 'We have invited this person today, to be a witness because we are afraid that you may act violently.'

4. Should the child become violent despite the presence of the witness, ask your guest to come into your child's room. Experience shows that the mere presence of a third party reduces the incidence of violence to near zero.

5. After the sit-in, continue with your daily household routine without referring to the sit-in or to its consequences.

Anticipating and preparing for your child's reaction

Your child will not like your entering his room and invading his space. Following is a series of scenarios that take into account possible reactions to the sit-in on the part of your child and the recommended parental responses:

ATTEMPTING TO EXPEL THE PARENT

The child will try expelling you from his room, for example by cursing or yelling 'Get out of here, I can't stand you!' This type of behaviour is best met with silence on your part. Do not be afraid that silence, on your part, would in any way mean that your dignity has been hurt.

> **Remember: it was you who engineered this sit-in and you continue to set the rules!**

Do not feel compelled to argue with your child; being drawn into an argument means you have lost the initiative and are now reacting to his provocation. The child may attempt to expel you, with physical violence – throwing things or pushing you out the door. When this situation occurs, defend yourself but do not attack your child. If you anticipate violence, make sure to invite a guest to the sit-in. Should your child begin acting in a violent way that can only be checked by your own display of force, stop the sit-in and leave his room, knowing you can begin again, any time you desire, and in the presence of witnesses. It is very important that you remain able to stop any action deemed highly escalatory. Here, you are required to use your common sense.

Remember: quitting any such action does not mean that you have given up. You retreat to regroup.

IMPOSING TERMS ON THE PARENTS

The child may attempt to stop the sit-in by imposing terms such as 'I'll do what you want if you buy me this or that.' Should this happen, say you cannot accept his offer, then go back to being silent again and await his further reaction.

IGNORING THE PARENTS

In ignoring you, your child is sending you the message that your actions have had no effect on him. He may turn on the television, stereo, or start up his computer. When this happens turn off the appliances, but do it only once. If the child decides to turn it back on, avoid further attempts and continue to sit until the sit-in is over.

Another type of reaction, meant to ignore your presence, is lying in bed pretending to be asleep. Time passes very slowly when the child pretends to be sleeping! Even if he has indeed fallen asleep, continue the sit-in without interruption. The child falling asleep while you're in his room signifies a change in attitude which can be taken to mean: 'I accept you staying in my room and offer you some measure of trust.' This is in contrast to anything the child might have said when awake.

TRYING TO EMBARRASS AND HUMILIATE THE PARENTS BY SHOUTING LOUDLY

In doing this, the child is trying to use the neighbours or other outside parties to interfere and stop the sit-in. If you expect this type of behaviour and are afraid of its repercussions, you may want to take the precaution of informing your neighbours about what is about to happen as well as the reasons for your planned actions. You may give them a copy of this guidebook.

TRYING TO PROVOKE THE PARENTS INTO SPEAKING

The child may attempt to lead you back to your old familiar role, where you continue to speak and he refuses to relate to what you are saying. He may do this by repeating for example: 'I don't understand what you want of me!' Alternatively, he may attempt to draw you into an argument. It is best not to respond but to maintain your silence. Any attempt to explain beyond your brief opening statement is an exercise in non-productive verbiage.

Accepting a positive offer made by the child

Ask the child about his offer, but only if it is concrete. An offer like 'I'll be a good boy!' requires clarification. When the child has come up with even a slight but realistic offer, end the sit-in and walk out of the room. Do not be afraid that the child has played you for a fool – if his behaviour does not improve you can always return to continue the sit-in.

It is important to realize that often children change their problematic behaviour without having made any offer during the sit-in. The sit-in is planned to affect both your child's behaviour and your own position in the family. Such effects occur whether your child has or has not made an offer. Should your child attempt to hold on to his dignity by refusing to make an offer, yet change his behaviour for the better, accept this as progress. The sit-in changes not only your child – it changes you as well. You discover that you are able to walk into your child's room and stay sitting there for as long as you have planned. You no longer let yourself be expelled, and you can avoid escalation. Most importantly, you learn that you carry personal and parental weight. Your place in the family has changed immeasurably.

The sit-in's purpose is to reduce the occurrence of problematic behaviour. Its purpose is not to have your child behave himself during the sit-in itself! Even if your child swears and curses at you throughout the sit-in, it does not mean that your action has been in vain. What determines the need for further sit-ins is the intensity of your child's problematic behaviours following the sit-in. Should you sense a diminishing of the problems, no further sit-ins will be needed. If on the other hand, you feel that problems are continuing, you must initiate further sit-ins.

THE 'TRANSPARENCY' PRINCIPLE: RECRUITING SUPPORTERS, MEDIATORS AND PUBLIC OPINION

One of the most important conditions for the success of your plan to resist your child's violent or destructive behaviour is to share the situation with others. The shroud of secrecy that hovers over the home characterizes families who are suffering from continuing violent situations. Experience shows that secrecy often feeds violence. Parents are naturally motivated to keep things quiet in order to protect themselves and their children. Yet in their desire to avoid being stigmatized, parents forgo all avenues of help and support – isolating themselves within the cycle of violence.

> **Remember: breaking the circle of silence and drawing on outside support hastens an end to the cycle of violence.**

You must draw a number of people into your confidence: friends and family members. Stop viewing your child's difficult behaviour as a close-kept secret. Make your child aware that the veil of silence has been lifted, that you are no longer alone. From now on things will be called for what they are – 'violence' or 'exploitation'.

TELEPHONE ROUNDS

'Telephone rounds' help restore both your presence and your supervision without resorting to violence. They are meant to demonstrate your disapproval of your child's disappearances and of his participation in certain activities. One of the possible responses your child may have to the conflict or to your attempts to change the status quo, is to disappear for hours at a time, overnight or even longer. A situation may also exist where the child will not bother to tell you where he is going and where he is hanging out. In order to effectively communicate your parental presence, you must pursue contact with your child even when he is away from home, by using the telephone or by using any other means.

Telephone rounds are telephone calls that you make that go round to every person your child keeps, or has kept, in touch with, in the event that he runs away or you don't know where he is. Telephone rounds serve to:

1. demonstrate parental presence and challenge the child's disappearances

2. locate the child

3. apply peer pressure to convince the child to come back home

4. bring the child back home.

The main purpose of doing the telephone rounds is not to bring the child back home. First and foremost, you must reassume the position of supervisor and you must fully restore your presence as a parent. Telephone rounds achieve all that even when you have not located your child! By doing the telephone rounds you leave your mark in many areas of your child's life. With each telephone call you expand your presence. You have passed on a message to him that you object to his disappearance and that you have expanded your network of support.

Telephone rounds reinforce the 'transparency' principle. Not only have you caused the child to return, you have proven that you are adamant about reaching out for help and about never again being alone to deal with your problems. This is a central tenet of the Non-Violent Resistance Model. In contacting others to show your parental concern, you promulgate the cause of your struggle. Therefore don't be surprised to find that you have won the support of parents who find themselves in similar circumstances to your own.

Collecting numbers

Step one in doing the telephone rounds is collecting the telephone numbers of your child's friends and acquaintances: other children, coaches, youth guides, club managers as well as the places you think that your child may be when away from home – sports club, video arcade, pub, disco. Gathering those numbers may be done using all available means and networking. For instance, you may ask a friend of your child, whose telephone number you already have, to give you telephone numbers of other friends that you do not have.

Calling and contacting

Step two is implemented either when your child is inexplicably late coming home, when he runs away or when he has disappeared. Should this occur you must call all the people and places on your prepared list. Be sure to call every number on your list, not only the places where you think you may find him. It is also important to continue your telephone rounds even after your child has been found – each number must be contacted! It is important to note that although you want to find your child, you also want to pass him the important message that you – his parents – are present wherever he may be. Calling your child on his mobile phone will not address the issue. On the contrary, your child turns off his mobile phone as a way of disappearing.

Speaking to your child's friends

Introduce yourselves; say that your child has disappeared and that you have been looking for him. Ask the friend to tell you if he has seen your child at school that day, if he has heard of your child's plans or if he has any idea where your child may be. Ask him to convey your concern to your child and to tell your child that you have been looking for him. Ask him if he could in any way convince your child to contact you.

This is a crucial moment in the conversation. According to his response, you will know if you have found someone who can act the part of mediator. If he is open to the possibility of offering you some assistance, try setting up a meeting between yourself and the friend. You have thus expanded your network of support to include some of your child's friends. This expansion may prove critical. When you finish with him, ask to speak with one of his parents.

Speaking to your child's friends' parents

Introduce yourselves in the same way that you have before and ask if they have seen your child lately. Ask them also not to let your child sleep over without your prior explicit consent. At times you will find willing allies in these parents, especially if they suffer similar problems. Try to meet with them – there is great potential in these parents' networks.

Speaking to the owners and employees of hangout spots

Ask them to try to locate your child on the spot, or at least give him a message that you are looking for him.

If it is too late to make telephone rounds, wait until the next day. Proceed with the telephone rounds even if you have located your child or if he has returned home. Be sure to tell everyone that your child was missing the previous night and that you were terribly worried. Ask them to tell you all they know and ask if they would be willing to help in the future, should he disappear again, to trace your child or otherwise convince him to get in touch with you. If your child protests that you needlessly embarrassed him (he is home after all), tell him that you have decided that you will no longer accept his disappearances. Apply to these telephone rounds the same rules which were mentioned before.

You will probably have located your child through telephone rounds. Another powerful tool you may choose to use is linking.

LINKING

The parental action of 'linking' is designed to minimize 'dead' spaces, that is unsupervised spaces, created by disappearances, unreported and unauthorized absences and by the child's other hidden activities. Linking is executed when parents search for their child and insist on appearing in those places deemed taboo for adults – places that may be dangerous including disco clubs, abandoned beaches or parks.

Studies have shown that children who can no longer be controlled detach themselves from their parents – a situation that may lead to deviation and to extreme and unusual behaviour by the child. Experience shows that detachment tends to be the result of some previous escalation, and in turn leads to further escalations. The purpose of linking, therefore, is not only to prevent problematic development caused by questionable unsupervised activities, but also to prevent the escalations caused by detachment itself. In other words, instead of reacting to the child's withdrawal by detaching yourself from your child – for instance by locking him out, or by angrily deciding to 'let the kid do what he wants!' or by instigating further escalation through the use of punishment and counter-punishment – you link. Linking enhances parental presence, acting to obstruct the process of detachment and deterring further escalation.

As with the other Non-Violent Resistance tools – sit-ins, telephone rounds, implementing the transparency principle, winning public opinion – linking will also cause your child to react in ways calculated to halt your parental action and to re-enact the old order of things by (a) attempting to create confrontation, and (b) attempting to further detach by running away or by shutting himself in.

To counter these reactions, you must carefully adhere to the principle of 'not being drawn in' and continue to resolutely maintain your supervision and contact with the child.

> **Repeat to yourself when faced with adversity: 'Abstain, never yield!'**

It is recommended that you link to your child under the following circumstances:

- When the child runs away from home: children often seek shelter with friends, extended family members, runaway shelters and among fringe groups defined as alternative youth cultures.

  Remember: although running away is regarded as an extreme reaction of the child, he continues to expect you – his parents – to come looking for him.

- When the child misses curfew or disappears for long hours during the day: in contrast to running away from home, which may be defined as an exceptional event indicating substantial turbulence, missing curfew and daily disappearances may be regarded as routine. The child thus comes to see them as 'basic rights' long awarded him by his parents. Consequently the child may show greater surprise and resistance at seeing his parents in his hangouts, than he might after running away from home.

- When the child spends time in questionable company who may be contributing towards his delinquency: it is generally believed that keeping bad company foretells one's decline. Gone unsupervised, your child may begin engaging in substance abuse, skipping school or taking part in delinquent and dangerous activities.

When linking, follow these rules:

1. Announce that you want your child back home and that he need not fear repercussions.

2. Avoid all arguments and whenever possible try to keep quiet while linking.

3. Avoid all physical actions that might lead to escalation – for example, grabbing your child and forcing him into your car.

4. Arrive at places frequented by your child and spend as much time as you can near him.

    Remember: the success of your linking is measured not by your ability to bring your child back, but by the power of your parental presence in resisting his detachment.

Forming a link may vary with the situation. Some examples are:

Linking while the child is at a friend's house

Ring the doorbell and say you have come to take your child home. If he comes forward, reassure him that you have no intention of punishing him but that you insist he come home with you. If he tries to evade you, say you are waiting for him. Ask his friend or his friend's parents, to let you wait inside the house. If you are not invited in, remain where you are and continue ringing the doorbell every ten minutes or so, asking that your child come home with you.

Linking when the child is hanging out on the street or at a club

Approach your child and let him know you expect him to come home with you and that you will not punish him. If he runs away – a typical reaction – do not chase after him. Instead, use the time to get to know his friends. Introduce yourself, ask them their names and for their telephone numbers and tell them about your difficult situation. Do not assume that they will oppose you; some may sympathize with your actions. During the conversation you might say: 'My child may be different from you. He may be putting himself in danger more often, as some of you may have more self-control than he does.' Or if your child's friends are older than he, if he is considered a rookie, you might say, 'You may already enjoy a greater degree of freedom. My kid is only 14!' or 'You may know when you've had enough, when it time to stop drinking, for instance. But I'm afraid, and maybe you have noticed yourself, that my child has little control over such things.'

Talking in this way may serve to build alliances, helping you find support where you least expected to find it. Some of these children may, in the future, play the crucial role of mediators. Friends recruited in this way have often brought back a runaway child.

Linking when your child has run away to join others his age who are living together for an unspecified period of time (in a commune, for instance)

Follow the previous instructions remembering that this time linking may take longer. In one case, for example, parents sat on the beach where young people lived for three days before their daughter, who had been missing from home for over a month, consented to come home with them.

Having a friend or family member join you while linking can be helpful in all the situations described above. It is good to have backup when visiting frightening locations where you think you may find your child – for example, when the child may be mingling in the company of drug dealers or users.

Linking's impact may be greater when you are accompanied. Your companion may be able to bridge the gap between you and your child, helping you find a suitable compromise, thus allowing your child to 'save face'.

> **Remember: you do not want to overpower your child.**
> **By simply having come and stayed, you have demon-**
> **strated parental presence.**

THE SIT-DOWN STRIKE

There are several aims to a 'sit-down strike':

1. appropriately responding to sharp escalations from your child, like running away from home or striking a parent

2. recruiting and demonstrating support for the parents and family

3. powerfully demonstrating parental presence.

A sit-down strike, in its make-up and content, may be described as a rite of passage. Rites of passage are meant to signal to individuals, family, and the community that life is at a crossroads. That is, that the situation known before the ritual will markedly differ from the situation following the ritual. The ritual itself is a symbolic event. Even more, it brings about new conditions that promote change in the behaviour of child and parent alike.

The preparations for a sit-down strike include:

1. Blocking off time: you must clear at least three full calendar days; it is possible to add one weekday to the weekend to make up these three days.

2. Inviting guests: try to contact as many friends, relatives and other people close to your child – teachers, youth guides, his friends and their parents – as possible. Describe your plans and the reasons behind them. You might say: 'We ask for your help in the wake of recent developments (*detail recent events*). Following this event X, we have decided to hold a three-day sit-down strike at our home. We are asking friends, family, and people who are close to our child to visit, to help us in trying to come up with a solution. We will be home with our child for all three days. Your presence is very important to us all!'

3. Should invitees make comments doubting the need for the strike, say: 'We are doing this because we are afraid of losing our child. We are seeking counsel and asking for help before it is too late!' Through their participation, guests become witnesses to and supporters of the parents' declaration that the situation cannot go on and requires immediate change. Some of the guests may take part in drafting a proposal or in executing practical or temporary solutions. They may lend a hand in helping the child with his studies, taking him out to exercise or having him over for the weekend or for a short holiday.

4. Preparing food: bringing food is a primary expression of support. It is recommended that friends and family bring food with them or cook for you while they visit. Those who cannot be present are asked at least to call and speak with the parents and to ask to speak with the child. Friends and family abroad may take part, using the telephone, fax or email.

Preparing your home for the event

Home preparations include:

- taking the keys to your child's bedroom so that he cannot lock himself in during the strike

- preparing food to last three days or asking close friends or relatives to bring food with them

- making yourself available to watch your child.

A central condition for the successful execution of a sit-down strike is maximum publicity. The extreme events preceding the strike justify breaking the bounds of discretion. Breaking silence constitutes a radical change in future family life, thus anointing the strike as a true rite of passage.

The sit-down strike begins when the child is at home and a small group of supporters is present (two to three people). It is recommended that you invite a friend of your child over too – one who has agreed to help you and your child find a way out of your present entanglement. The presence of one of his friends helps diminish polarization, which could occur if only your friends are present.

Your announcement marks the opening of the event: 'We have decided to hold a three-day sit-down strike in order to reach a solution to recent event X (*describe the event*). During these three days we will all stay at home. People who wish to help us will visit. We will not work nor entertain ourselves nor will we leave this house. (*Your child's name*) will remain with us. We will not chastise you nor punish you. Whatever solution we reach, it will not include punishing you, for that is not our purpose. We simply want our family to find its way out of this situation.' If you cannot impart this message directly to your child, ask a mediator to convey the message to him.

What happens if your child tries to leave the house?

You should try to stop your child from leaving the house, even if it means locking the house door. Should the child leave the house any-way, continue the strike as planned while conducting a wide circle of telephone rounds. Once you have located your child, start linking with the help of your supporters. Insofar as it is possible, one parent should continue the strike at home while the other links. In single parent households, one guest should remain at home to play host to the visi-tors. Should your child refuse to speak with you or with your guests, continue the strike as planned, asking your guests to greet your child upon entering and to write him a farewell note before leaving. Small parting gifts for the child are also welcome – a symbolic item such as a greeting card, a flower or a favourite food or treat. These gifts are considered as gestures of reconciliation from the 'outside world'. Do not try to force your child to communicate under any circumstances.

What happens if your child hurls accusations and humiliates you in front of your guests at the sit-down strike?

Should the child vociferously accuse his parents of aggression, com-pulsion, humiliation or treachery, they must reply in person or via mediators, 'We have no intention of punishing or humiliating you, nor have we any intention of overpowering you. It is our supreme duty to act as we do, as we find ourselves compelled by this intolerable situa-tion.' On this, guests must stand by the parents, helping them convey their message concisely. If your child is willing to communicate with a small group of people or even with just one person, they/he/she must become the mediator(s). The mediator's role is to bridge the gap between parent and child while avoiding the assignment of blame to both parties. The mediator must also have come to the conclusion that 'the present situation is intolerable and must not be allowed to continue'. The mediator's suggestions will be discussed by the parents and put to the consideration of guests who are present or friends who can be reached by phone.

How do you end the sit-down strike?

By no means should the strike end with threats or sanctions. It is best to conclude it in writing, by thanking those who have come for their friendship and support. Convey your thoughts in writing to everyone, including your child. These thoughts should not take the form of an agreement that your child signs. Rather, there must be a written account which briefly describes the whole rite of passage.

Ask your guests to continue calling the family and the child in the weeks following the strike. After a big event like a sit-down strike, you might think that in the future, your responses to your child's difficult behaviour must be on the same grandiose level. This is not the case. Your response to his behaviour should remain within the normal measures of Non-Violent Resistance (sit-ins, telephone rounds, the Non-Violent Resistance Model and reconciliation). However, the strike has now created a new reality, which allows the parent to operate within the supporting reach of friends and extended family.

DISOBEDIENCE: REFUSING ORDERS

'Refusing orders' is a step of Non-Violence Resistance where the parents: (1) refuse to carry out actions which they have felt compelled to perform in the past, for example, giving out spending money, chauffeuring, etc.; (2) reinstate important activities which they have been prevented from carrying out in the past, for example, entering the child's room, checking or putting his belongings in order when necessary. The parents thus signal their termination of obedience patterns, patterns which perpetuate escalation.

Refusing orders has a number of aims:

1. to terminate parental yielding patterns

2. to make parents aware of the services they provide and challenge the child not to take these services for granted

3. to provide the parents a wider range of possibilities of reaching their child.

While sit-ins, telephone rounds and sit-down strikes prove suitable answers to extreme events, refusing orders is best suited to routine circumstance. Your child has become used to being chauffeured, to being served upon demand, to his food being prepared just the way he likes it, to the television being turned to his favourite shows, etc. The purpose of refusing orders is to shake the foundations of the unbalanced, intolerable reality taken as an absolute given by the child.

In trying to follow the development of situations such as this, one may assume that over the years some gradual unfelt process has turned you from parents who can say 'no' to some of your child's demands, into parents completely obedient to your child's every whim. Through this process, your freedom of action has been dramatically narrowed, while your child's freedom to display his disruptive behaviour has continued to expand.

As you have been 'trained' to follow his will, so he has grown less sensitive to yours. Eventually, you come to regard yourselves as 'patsies' subject to his wants and unable to disobey. The intention of refusing orders is to liberate you from feeling abused and oppressed. By refusing orders you discover that this abnormal situation cannot exist without your consent. You will also discover that you never truly consented, but have given away your rights of consent under the implicit or explicit threat of being punished by your child.

> **Remember: refusing orders is not an attempt to punish your child, but to break your patterns of obedience, and thus uncover your own will and voice as parents.**

Refusing orders may proceed on two complementary planes:

- 'Service strike': stopping all services given to your child under explicit or implicit duress.

- 'Breaking taboo': conducting parental activities which have until now been forbidden by your child.

Service strike

In order to prepare, you must assess and re-evaluate all the services you provide to your child. Try to distinguish between services provided willingly and unnecessary services provided under duress. Services provided under your child's coercion are frequently associated with the demand implicitly or explicitly expressed: 'Do this or I will...' followed by some threat.

The parents then choose which of those imposed services to stop. Some examples of services which parents choose to include in their strikes are: driving the child to classes, friends or parties, luxury foods or drinks, demands for particular dishes, metered services such as mobile phones which the child uses indiscriminately, or any command deemed unreasonable to you. The stronger the child's demands for a particular service, the more likely that it was given unwillingly.

> **Remember: the more loudly the child demands the service, the more likely that it fits the category of services that should be put on strike!**

The conduct and aims of this strike differ radically from the conduct and aims of punishments:

- The reason a service is put on strike is not that the child has behaved badly, rather, it is the parents' realization that such service is not given of their free will but given by them under the child's duress.

- Services will not be restored once the child behaves well. (Parents may restore certain services if they wish once they are convinced that the threat attached to the service and their reaction to it has been removed.)

- While punishment is meant to alter the child's behaviour, the strike seeks to reverse the parents' self-opinion and terminate their patterns of obedience, putting an end to their feelings of being used. The strike may very well contribute to improving the child's behaviour but that achievement stands secondary to the change sought in the parents' self-worth and in their enhanced parental presence.

Remember: the service strike is not a punishment!

Breaking taboo

In preparing for this action, you must identify areas of your life at home where free access and movement have been severely limited. Such common taboos are: restricted access to your child's room, restrictions on inviting guests – either who you invite or when you invite them, inability to arrange your home according to your taste, restricted television viewing in the living room, limited telephone access and more.

Perhaps your friends and family have in the past directed your attention to your over-accommodating acceptance of certain restrictions from your child. Those areas of obedience are perfect for breaking taboo. When you have decided which taboo to break, inform those who have previously identified this problem and other potential supporters of your decision.

Anticipating your child's reaction

Expect that in this area too your child will try to break your resistance using threats, violence or accusations. According to previously taught principles, your response must be: abstain and do not yield! Moreover, you may choose to respond by employing various Non-Violent Resistance tools. For instance, in response to violence you may initiate a sit-in to mobilize public support. In response to running away, you may initiate telephone rounds, etc.

Telling your child in advance of your refusal to carry out orders

Inform your child in a discreet and calm manner. Take care to steer away from the implication or threat of the 'I am the boss!' stance. Simply tell your child calmly, 'I will no longer do X.' Do not explain yourself, do not try to justify or argue – all of that will ultimately lead to escalation.

By means of refusing orders and breaking taboo you have stopped automatically obeying your child and have regained your decision-making power. That sense of freedom felt immediately upon disobeying, will help empower you in your continuing struggle to overcome the extreme and disruptive behaviour of your child. The forearmed parent, who no longer obeys, is able to change not only the atmosphere at home, but also his own sense of self. Refusing orders leads to a substantial re-evaluation of the parents' self-worth.

At the end of this process, you will be able to reinstate some of the services which you terminated, perhaps driving your child from time to time, letting him have his own mobile phone, etc. Reinstatement, however, depends not only upon your child's behaviour but principally upon your wish. You must ask yourself: 'Am I sure that there are no threats attached? Do I really want to reinstate this service? Will I feel free to withhold the service if the circumstances change?'

Such investigation takes into account the parents alone, not the child. Termination and/or reinstatement of services depend upon you.

RECONCILIATION

In order that conflicts and power struggles do not become the axis around which your relationship with your child revolves, it is vital to perform 'acts of reconciliation'. Studies in escalation prove that reconciliatory acts greatly diminish escalatory threats. Reconciliatory acts minimize resentment at home, helping to build a broader, more positively based relationship. Reconciliatory acts should not be conditional upon the actions and behaviour of your child – they are not to be taken as rewards nor should the child be punished by withholding them. By giving, acts of reconciliation enable you to become loving parents again, while simultaneously continuing your unyielding struggle of Non-Violent Resistance.

> **Remember: acts of reconciliation do not replace Non-Violent Resistance – they complement it.**

The main avenues of reconciliation are:

- **Words: verbal or written**

    Say and write things that are respectful of your child, his talents, his attributes and his world view. Show him that you appreciate and respect that he pursues what is important to him.

- **Treats: preparing his favourite meal or buying his favourite foods**

    Do not insist that your child accept what you have prepared. If you have cooked his favourite meal, do not be adamant that he eats it right away and that he eats it with you. Treats are unconditional gestures of giving, from you to your child. Your child will choose his own way to accept or refuse them. Avoid giving expensive items/services. Certainly do not give anything that the child demands as a pre-condition to improving his behaviour.

- **Mending**

    A meaningful gesture may be to fix the child's favourite toy or a favourite household item that he broke during a fit of anger.

Repairing an object symbolizes repairing the relationship. Do not be afraid of being perceived as weak.

Remember: you do not want to be seen as all powerful, in overcoming your child. You want to be seen as caring parents!

• **Suggesting positive family activities**

For example, walking together, going to a movie together, engaging together in sports or exercise or participating in some other regular activity he enjoys.

Remember: he is allowed to refuse without 'losing points'.

• **Expressing remorse**

A very special reconciliatory act is expressing regret over some past parental act of aggression. Parents tend to shy away from expressing their regret, for fear of being considered weak.

Remember: acts of reconciliation go hand in hand with the actions of Non-Violent Resistance.

There is little chance your child will interpret them as signs of weakness. Most likely, he will accept them for what they truly are: voluntary attempts at reconciliation. Acts of reconciliation express your heartfelt desire to expand your relationship with your child beyond the narrow confines of difficult encounters and power struggles.

How will your child respond to the acts of reconciliation?

It is likely that your child will initially reject your attempts at reconciliation. However, rejection does not mean you have failed in your initiative. Your child is simply trained by habit to arbitrarily defer all your advances. In spite of his rejection, your actions are truly worthwhile as they help to consolidate and project your positive presence as parents in your child's life. Do not relent in your attempts to reconcile with your child – even when he rejects you.

Remember: you must not force him to accept your gestures – just keep trying.

SUMMARY: EMPOWERMENT AND READINESS

The means and tools of Non-Violent Resistance that we have described are designed to empower you. The various techniques presented were not randomly assembled. Non-Violent Resistance is not materialized by simply holding a sit-in or by picking up the phone to do the telephone rounds. The process becomes powerful only when assembling and fusing the tools with the principles.

The actions at your disposal are:

- *declaring* that you no longer accept the present situation

- *breaking silence* and gathering support

- *asking supporters* to let the child know that they have been informed of his behaviour

- *sit-ins*

- *telephone rounds*

- *linking*

- *finding allies* among your child's friends and their parents

- *sit-down strikes*

- *refusing orders*: ending all extorted services and breaking taboo

- *acts of reconciliation*

- *never yielding*

- *not being drawn in* to potentially escalatory behaviour.

One action reinforces the next. Focusing on the task at hand, you prove to yourselves and to your child that life at home has radically changed. Preparing yourself for this task requires resolve, a strong sense of responsibility and moral fortitude. In order to guarantee success, you must assign top priority to Non-Violent Resistance. Experience shows that you need three months of full focus, to have an impact. Once this period is over, the situation will have irreversibly changed. You will discover that being alert requires less and less effort on your part, because you have developed new habits. What characterized you in the past – yielding and being unable to abstain from involvement – gradually becomes foreign and irrelevant. When your child tries to provoke you, he does not elicit your old patterned reactions. The new situation brings with it a deep-felt change in your home and in your relationship with your child.

In order to reach this level, you must resist the illusion of achieving immediate results. Parents who expect change after just one or two sit-ins will inevitably be disappointed.

> **Parents be advised: until you have invested a significant amount of time in practical, focused parental presence – sitting-in, making telephone rounds, building support, linking, etc. – you have not been fully enlisted.**

However, once this initial effort has been made, you will notice your child's first signs of accommodation. At times you may doubt just how much the situation with your child has changed. These doubts can be useful and are certainly justified. Do not be complacent. Do not assume that your child has already internalized things, that he has found a new path. Deep-felt changes are happening within you! You are learning to respond differently, think differently, and slowly starting to feel differently! As these changes take root within you, your child's potential for risky, destructive behaviour will inevitably decrease.

In becoming resilient, you must steel yourself for your child's tough reactions. You cannot expect a child accustomed to power and independence, to simply give it all away. Your child will do everything to convince you that your efforts are fruitless, that you have no chance of success, and that by acting as you do you are only making things worse. Your child will want you to surrender and be drawn into conflict again and again.

If in the past he was capable of derailing you – of making you surrender, of involving you in conflict by arguing, by throwing insults or curses, by threatening, by playing the victim, by worrying you or inducing guilt in you – he will inevitably try it again!

> **Remember: yielding and being drawn into conflict will set you back. Be especially vigilant and aware of the dangers of being drawn into violent outbursts – verbal or physical. Each of those violent outbursts can take days to heal.**

Guard yourself against these reactions by implementing the following principles:

1. Expect and prepare for your child's hard-hitting reactions. Your position is much stronger if you are not caught by surprise. In that case, although things may still be difficult, they are at least tolerable.

2. Extreme reactions are short-lived. Your child will not continue escalating his response forever. The more extreme his reaction, the shorter it will last. When you do not yield, when you continue to refrain from being drawn into conflict, your child's harsh reactions will lose their hold. Without your reactions, his reactions are denied the 'fuel' required for escalation.

3. Call upon your supporters to help you absorb and withstand your child's tough reactions. Aside from the obvious support they provide, recruiting friends and family members to help steel you against your child's reactions can transmit the message to your child that you have resolved to maintain your new course.

4. Employ mediators to mitigate crises. Among your supporting friends and family, find mediators who are able to communicate with your child. This special contact will help to ease your child's sense of loneliness and may help to preserve his dignity in addition to moderating his responses.

Remember, above all: yielding to your child's behaviour guarantees escalation. By contrast, maintaining your presence as parents and adhering to the principles of the Non-Violent Resistance Model, protects your relationship with your child, shields him from the disruptive effects of his own behaviour and enables you to best protect him from harm. Ultimately, the Non-Violent Resistance Model serves to empower you to fully resume your natural role as a parent and allows your child to revert to his natural role as your child.

CHAPTER ELEVEN

Overview

Reports about the phenomenon of violent and coercive relationships between children and parents abound and are increasing with time. There is significant public debate surrounding the issue, specifically around whether it is indeed what it is being made out to be. Is this problem not inherent to the parent–child relationship? Is the exponential growth merely a result of increased media coverage? In a world of quick, easy media access, has this problem – as well as many other problems present in modern life – gained artificial volume? Is the increased incidence of violence and coercion in parent–child relations a product of the rapid and fundamental changes in modern society? Why do so many parents and educators, when seeking professional advice in coping with this phenomenon, minimize what they see, relegating it to an isolated incident? Is this a reflection of their deep apprehension at facing this frightening reality?

Whatever the case may be, children exhibiting destructive behaviour on the one hand, and overwhelmed, distressed parents and educators on the other hand, have become commonplace. They cross the spectrum of social and cultural landscapes – it is no longer a phenomenon relegated to underprivileged families, as is seen in the literature[1] as well as the case studies presented in this book. All families are vulnerable and can reach a state which seems beyond repair or *therapy resistant*, as it is referred to in professional literature.

As we have mentioned earlier, psychotherapy for children who display severe behavioural problems poses a great challenge, especially with regards to adolescents. Very often, in spite of the best of efforts, therapy does not result in change or improvement. In fact, a drop-out

---

1   See Dagenais, D. (2008) *The (Un)Making of the Modern Family*, trans. J. Brierley. Vancouver: UBS Press.

rate sometimes reaching 70 per cent is common. Drop-out is primarily due to two reasons: (1) Simply that the children or adolescents refuse to co-operate. (2) Parents who are struggling with extremely difficult circumstances are exhausted and drained and cannot keep up the process. In previous chapters, we described the range of behaviours in such children. We found that such children experienced difficulty in adjusting at school and at home, and very often engaged in troubled, coercive and violent relationships with peers and family. The suffering and distress is substantial on both sides – parents and children are mutually affected.

Our work was driven to meet the challenge of creating a working model to effectively coach parents, affording them efficient, practical and manageable procedures to reach the goal of preserving a healthy parent–child relationship and facilitating the healthy growth and development of the child.

The model of Non-Violent Resistance and the intervention were designed to meet the growing need for a viable answer to those complications and difficulties that are inherent to extremely troubled relations between parents and children, like those described in the case studies. Our main focus evolved around the idea that even in the worst cases, where the relationship between child and parent seems to reach the point of no return, the possibility of healing is still feasible. Thus, we began our work on the model, asking the question, 'How can we bring about change?' This question of how to bring about change is the core of the model presented in this book. Our focus is the formation of the initial change, the catalyst from which development and healing emerge.

In the previous chapters, we illustrated the theory and practice of the Non-Violent Resistance Model through six study cases. All except one were enacted and thoroughly examined within the framework of the research project. All pointed clearly to the promise and potential of the model, as it materialized through our work. We demonstrated how the prospect for success lies in creating the prerequisite conditions that enable willingness for treatment, and motivate commitment to adhere to change. Those conditions are: soothing the situation, being present and monitoring, taking responsibility for the child/situation at all times. When the voice of violence in all its forms is silenced, the demonstrated procedures help to bring to the surface the hidden psychological and social issues of the individuals involved – parents and children. We observed that when the situation is soothed, the treatment can begin.

In our studies, we invested great efforts in establishing our method scientifically, and the results indeed proved to validate the method. However, we would like to posit that the crux of a successful intervention, as seen in the pervious chapters, lies to a great extent in a change of heart on the part of the parents and the other participants.

We went to great lengths to describe both the mechanisms and conditions that fuel destructive behaviour in children. Contrary to conventional practice, we did not dwell on the child. The parent is the one who received our full attention. As we pointed out in the second chapter, removing the child from the equation makes the intervention possible. Success in modifying the problematic dynamic is not expected to be generated through the child or by the child. The child's behaviour or the child's willingness to participate no longer dictates whether the parent can act successfully to regain presence in the child's life. Thus, the parent reclaims his responsibility for the child. The parent is now present and back in the centre of the child's life.

As essential as parental presence is, so is the acknowledgement of parental suffering. Parents are treated respectfully for enduring the suffering caused by the child's difficult behaviour. To be a parent is never easy, let alone to be a parent of a child who challenges every fibre of the parent's being. Add to that poor health, loneliness, the struggle to maintain a job, to generate adequate income, marital problems, single parenthood; and we may just get a sense as to how tough and demanding it can be to be a parent of such a child.

At the same time, we encourage parents to own up to the mistakes made towards the child, as well as to clearly articulate their intention to do all that it takes to heal the wounds. This stand does not detract from the parents' central role and their ability to make a difference in the child's life. On the contrary, as evidenced by the case studies, it enables parent and child to begin to rewrite their shared family experience.

In this way, the parent is freed from guilt. The focus shifts from the fault of the parents to the power of the parents – they hold the key to the solution. The parent is called to step up and reclaim his natural role. The parent is called to be present at all times. The parent is called to maintain an ongoing dialogue with his environment. As we have seen, this dialogue produces two important things: it maintains the necessary transparency so fundamental to the process of change, and it provides the social support that fortifies parental presence and lends it reinforced legitimacy. Whereas beforehand the parent was viewed as the cause for failure and malfunctioning in the child, we choose to address the parent as a resourceful individual who can model inner beliefs about his own abilities. As such, the parent is empowered to shape and influence his child's present and future and enhance his prospects for success.

FEAR AND STATUS QUO

One of the greatest fears of parents in implementing the model is the implications of radical change in the status quo of parent–child relations. Parents fear that imposing clear boundaries and limiting freedoms previously enjoyed by the child, will escalate the situation further, damaging the little affection remaining between them. The data gathered in our study on escalation and affection proves that such fear is unfounded. Indeed, we found that the child's level of affection remains the same throughout the intervention. This result allays the parents' fears. In addition, it demonstrates the model's efficacy in reducing escalation while restraining problematic behaviour – with no negative consequence.

Asking family-based questions reveals itself not only as a tool for data collection on escalation but as a tool to further the goals of the intervention itself. The official sessions are informed by data, focusing the work around specific events. This enhances the feeling of concretization, of planning and efficacy, adding a definite, objective dimension that is intertwined with the therapy. Therefore, asking about levels of escalation and affection in the parent–child interaction becomes an awareness-enhancing tool, sensitizing parents to distinguishing nuances in their child's behaviour. It not only enables parents to differentiate between negative behaviours of varying character and intensity but also helps them recognize the existence of other behaviours such as manifestation of affection. Most importantly, it sensitizes them and enables them to clearly locate their own contribution, as parents, to the cycle of escalation (Aldridge 1984, 1988, 1999) without apportioning blame. Our decision to use the mother's report was based on the fact that in most families, the mother was the main care-taker. The process of ongoing verification takes place throughout the intervention by means of the input of partners, school officials and friends/mediators. Thus the mother's report resonates with many different sources.

The ideas presented above may raise a question on the objectivity of such report. Does the mother's report accurately reflect the objective occurrences at home, or does it reflect the mother's wish to portray herself and her efforts positively? Many of the parents report during the sessions that just knowing that at the end of the day the care team member would call to collect the data, strengthens their resolve to insist on adhering to the principles of action agreed upon in the intervention. Furthermore, they report that the anticipated call of the care team member often helps them to restrain themselves from losing control. This may indicate that the mother's report is coloured by her need to portray herself in a positive light.

In accordance with Aldridge and Rossiter (1984), we traced details of difficult episodes asking parents step-by-step questions such as: 'What happened?' 'Who was present?' 'What was said?' and 'Then what happened?' Our focus here is not on the number or frequency of escalatory episodes but primarily on the nature of such episodes.

This approach helps to:

- shift the focus from the individual, the child, to those who are instrumentally involved in the situation – the family or significant others

- shed light on understanding the other participants' roles in the situation

- point to the possible existence of a message with a repeated pattern that is handled in a certain way in the system, i.e. the family or those living under the same roof

- discover whether the episode in question occurred as an event in a sequence of social interaction or as an isolated event

- move away from an emotional perspective to a sequential, consequential behavioural perspective.

THE GUIDEBOOK FOR PARENTS

The *Guidebook for Parents* (see Chapter 10) was designed to introduce parents to the fundamental principles associated with the Non-Violent Resistance Model as well as to the work tools designed to apply those principles.

Parents are encouraged to review the guide, especially when the situation with the child seems particularly overwhelming. Reading the *Guidebook* serves as a catalyst for an animated dialogue between the parents and the care team and between the parents themselves. It facilitates a process of introspection, allowing parents to examine their old accepted moral stands and perceptions.

The ideas presented in the *Guidebook* elicit resistance from some parents. Parents who were characterized by an authoritarian discipline style find the ideas too liberal in their demand to categorically abstain from all forms of violent reactions towards the child, both physical and verbal. They may also have difficulty with its recommendation to avoid an immediate reaction to the child's aggressive or coercive behaviour. They agree even less with the notion that parents should take reconciliation steps irrespective of a noticeable change in their child's behaviour.

Parents characterized by a permissive discipline style find it difficult to agree with some of the recommended tools such as: sit-ins, telephone rounds, the sit-down strike and refusing orders. Their initial response is that these methods are too invasive and that they ignore the child's right to privacy. At times, when each partner espouses a different parenting style, criticism on either side is voiced.

One set of issues that is particularly problematic for all parents, regardless of their parental style, is disclosure, transparency and public opinion. Initially, most parents insist that revealing the ongoing reality at home to the outside world will harm child and family alike. Parents characterized by an authoritarian discipline style are primarily concerned with the damage to the image of the child as well as to the family. On the other hand, parents with a permissive discipline style are more concerned that conveying the problem to the outside world will in effect betray the child.

With regard to perceived social support, female participants manage to overcome these obstacles more easily than their male counterparts, ultimately generating the necessary support and translating this into their own sense of enhanced self-efficacy.

An intensive therapeutic dialogue developed around the principles of Non-Violent Resistance, addressing the whole concept of challenging escalation and aggression with non-violent means. From the parents' consent to adopt the model's reasoning, to translating that reasoning into a plan of action tailored to that particular family's needs – all of this evolved naturally from the therapeutic dialogue with each family. Within the overall time frame of therapeutic intervention, an individualized pace was set for each family to activate the tools proposed by the model.

In retrospect, however, parents of young children found the *Guidebook for Parents* only partially useful as its particular design and tools are geared towards parents of school age children and teenagers. An adaptation of the tools for a younger age group is not provided in the *Guidebook*. In each of the cases where parents sought intervention for their young child, the tools presented in the *Guidebook* were adapted to suit their particular case.

Principally, the work with parents of young children emphasizes the shift from a 'time-out' (Cavell 2001) technique to a 'time-in' technique. This technique postulates that the child should not be sent to remain alone. Instead, in keeping with the idea of parental presence, the parent takes the child with him to another room, telling him they will both spend some time together until the child calms down. After that, the child is free to return to where he came from and what he was doing. This is to be enacted by parents whenever their child acts out. This 'time-in' principle remains, for no particular reason, unformulated. To answer this need, a work is in process designed specifically for the younger child that elaborates on this vital principle, and provides relevant examples.

The discourse on parental authority in the professional literature warns of the possible dangers involved in advocating methods designed to enhance parental authority and parental power (Cavell 2001). Their warnings are based on the notion that these methods might be interpreted by parents – especially parents with a harsh discipline style – as a reason to be even harsher than they were before the intervention. To counter such possibilities, the above discussion reinforces that the *Guidebook* is only to be used with the guidance and supervision of a qualified therapist.

The vital discourse that evolves from reading the *Guidebook* points not only to its utility but to the caution necessary when utilizing it.

THE SITUATION, NOT THE CHILD

Much of the research in the field uses the expression of 'soothing the child'. In contrast, the Non-Violent Resistance Model aims at 'soothing the situation'. This difference in wording most aptly emphasizes the difference between the operative model of Non-Violent Resistance and the other existing models. Soothing the situation implies relieving the distress of all participants. Here parent and child are given the possibility of engaging in different and other forms of interaction, rather than perpetuating the familiar escalation cycle. In many cases once the intervention was over, children agreed to therapy and parents were ready to look more closely at their marital relationship or to examine individual issues that had surfaced during the intervention. It was thus apparent that the intervention could also serve as a preparatory stage for deeper and more specific individual work – for the parent, for the child, for the parent–child relationship or for the parents' relationship.

This book demonstrates that parents' reports are relevant and contribute to the task, that being the measuring of anti-social behaviour. If the parents' role is to be effectively restored, then it is appropriate and even necessary to allow the parents to voice their knowledge and their beliefs about the child, whatever they may be. This notion resonates with Non-Violent Resistance's ideology and mission. In assessing the problem, the move from a micro to a macro system plays a vital role that extends far beyond the assessment task itself. Forming an eco-systemic perspective creates opportunities for the parent or child to cultivate a broader perspective and creates channels for new forms of personal, familial and social interaction.

The opportunities presented here not only offer a solid base for the individual, but also serve to protect the quality of transparency so essential to any process of change, healing and development.

The particular concept of change employed here is based on a minimal intervention. The achieved change in the cycle of escalation allows the participants to identify specific problem areas, thereby opening up opportunities for targeted change.

ESCALATION AS STAGNATION

The Non-Violent Resistance Model operates on two levels. Escalation is targeted not as a symptom but as a problem and the problem is located within a wider social ecology. The Non-Violent Resistance world view maintains that the individual needs to associate himself with a moral statement about his life and his existential state. The voicing of such a statement to himself and to others enables the individual to remain engaged in the process of change, progressively taking concrete steps towards improvement. The need to express and reframe the individual's existential state appeared to be a *leitmotiv* recurring in the work that unfolded with most of the parents.

On the surface escalation can easily be confused with movement, whereas in truth it reflects stagnation. Family therapists used to refer to this as 'more of the same'. The movement of escalation goes round in circles becoming more intense, but the movement in real change is linear – progressing from one point to the next. As in any expression of change, the reframing and rephrasing of the individual's suffering can create a delicate but deeply significant movement in the individual's perception of his state and place in the world.

Support reveals itself to be a key concept associated essentially with the individual's existential-moral statement of self. The answers to questions like: 'Who are the people I know?' 'With whom do I have contact?' 'From whom can I expect or seek help?' appear to be a cardinal aspect of the parent's identity.

MOTHERS AND FATHERS: A MUTUAL APPRECIATION OF GENDER ROLES IN PARTNERSHIP

Much has been written on the different role of men and women in their children's lives, on the willingness of men to participate in the process of problem solving and on their tendencies to avoid or ignore that clear necessity. In the course of work with the families, typically fathers refuse to play an active role – apart from attending the sessions. Alternatively, some fathers espouse a somewhat disapproving and critical attitude towards the process.

However, once the mother is brought to the realization that the father is indispensable and that certain attitudes and exchanges are responsible for his engaging or disengaging with the process – a new dialogue is created. This dialogue emphasizes the central role of mutual appreciation of the other partner's importance, ability and indispensability in attaining the intervention's proposed goals.

According to the Non-Violent Resistance Model, participation involves a full recruitment – not only attending the sessions but being committed to and engaging with the process dynamically. Refraining from emphasizing the lack of ability in the other partner, cultivates an exchange on the legitimate needs – existential and practical – of each partner.

The Non-Violent Resistance Model stresses the importance of the father's role in the success of the intervention. Vital to that success, however, is the attempt to consider how to overcome his lack of interest, resentment and cynicism from past experience, and subsequent lack of belief in the process.

In all three stages, it is apparent that the successful enlistment of fathers in the process, plays a vital role. It is often the case that next to a helpless mother, a father appears in need of protection from the mother's anger at being left alone to face the difficulties of the child's behaviour. At times, it seems that the father is assigned this position unwittingly by the mother or simply by the circumstances of his life. Along with recognizing the mother's vulnerabilities, the therapeutic stand of the Non-Violent Resistance intervention equally recognizes the father's vulnerability. The co-operation between mother and father is ultimately, if not primarily, intended to protect the vulnerability of each one. The intervention is successful in maintaining a dialogue that assigns mutual importance to both parents and cultivating compassion for the lack of abilities and limitations of the other partner, as is evidenced by the low drop-out rate.

Our aim is not to treat the couple's relationship, nor the individual's existential problems *per se*, but to view and understand how the spectrum of various roles meet and interact to serve and maintain escalatory relationships within the family system, especially with regard to the child with behavioural problems. This aim has to be pursued with utmost caution according to the basic moral position of Non-Violent Resistance which is: respect for the other and compassion for the lack of abilities of the other. These two principles constitute that dialogue, enabling it to progress to the next level of identifying what has failed and what needs to be mended and healed.

TAKING RESPONSIBILITY, NOT APPORTIONING BLAME

A common hindrance to any therapeutic dialogue aimed at counselling parents – on the part of the therapist as well as the parent – is the confusion of blame and responsibility.

The principles propagated by the Non-Violent Resistance Model help overcome this hindrance by assuring the parent of protection during the course of the intervention; respect for his knowledge and understanding of his child; acknowledgement of his capability in providing his child with good care; and empathy for his lack of knowledge, skills or abilities. It is human to be found wanting. It is also a human capacity to learn new abilities and create new solutions.

The principles involved in this therapeutic stand enable the parent to relinquish blame and to assume responsibility, allowing the parent to transcribe this into a commitment to a new process of change.

PLANNED PARENTAL ACTION

This model deliberately promotes those elements referred to in the literature as the 'placebo aspect in psychotherapy'. However, these elements are implemented with the utmost care to maintain a realistic balance by constantly emphasizing that the action taken will not necessarily result in noticeable change in the child; being vigilant to the appearance of possible complications; focusing on the difficulty involved in enduring the process; and attaching importance to the parents' subjective expression of their suffering. These emphases create the platform that enables the parents to face the next difficult episode with the child, moving them to the next level of planned parental action and fortifying them to endure the entire process.

A note to therapists: all of us share the aspiration of positively impacting on the life of our client, to the extent that the client regains his emotional health. However, we see that the core of therapy, especially as seen in the cases studies given earlier, is to establish the initial change. This initial change is the first step that directs the rest of the work. It is from here that therapy can begin.

The Non-Violent Resistance Model, rooted in the eco-systemic world view, is open to different interpretations in the way that it is implemented. The ideal goal of the therapist is to interpret, to accommodate, to adjust and to fine-tune the concepts and the language of the Non-Violent Resistance Model to the language, rules and beliefs of the particular family in question. The fact that the model's ideas are constantly open to interpretation makes it robust, versatile and flexible to each familial constellation, restoring both parental power and a healthy child–parent relationship in a family system that allows children to be children and parents to be parents.

References

Aldridge, D. (1984) 'Family interaction and suicidal behaviour: A brief review.' *Journal of Family Therapy 6,* 3, 309–322.

Aldridge, D. (1988) 'Treating self-mutilating behaviour: A social strategy.' *Family System Medicine 6,* 1, 5–20.

Aldridge, D. (1999) *Suicide: The Tragedy of Hopelessness.* London and Philadelphia: Jessica Kingsley Publishers.

Aldridge, D. and Rossiter, J. (1984) 'A strategic assessment of deliberate self-harm.' *Journal of Family Therapy 6,* 2, 113–129.

Avraham-Krehwinkel, C. (2003) 'Non-violent resistance – a new approach to violent and self-destructive children.' Paper presented at the Second Research Symposium conducted at the Faculty of Medicine, Witten/Herdecke University, Witten/Herdecke, Germany. (In German.)

Avraham-Krehwinkel, C. (2005) *Non-Violent Resistance as a Coping Approach for Parents of Children with Disruptive Behaviours: Establishing a Viable Research Instrument.* Unpublished doctoral dissertation at the Faculty of Medicine, Witten/Herdecke University, Germany.

Bandura, A. (1969) *Principles of Behavior Modification.* New York, NY: Holt, Rinehart and Winston.

Bandura, A. (1973) *Aggression: A Social Learning Analysis.* Englewood Cliffs, NJ: Prentice-Hall.

Bates, J.E., Bayles, K., Bennett, D.S., Ridge, B. and Brown, M.M. (1991) 'Origins of Externalizing Behavior Problems at Eight Years of Age.' In D. Pepler and K. Rubin (eds) *Development and Treatment of Childhood Aggression.* Hillsdale, NJ: Lawrence Erlbaum.

Bates, J.E., Freeland, C.A.B. and Lounsbury, M.L. (1979) 'Measurement of infant difficultness.' *Child Development 50,* 794–803.

Bates, J.E., Pettit, G.S. and Dodge, K.A. (1995) 'Family and Child Factors in Stability and Change in Children's Aggressiveness in Elementary School.' In J. McCord (ed.) *Coercion and Punishment in Long-term Perspectives.* New York, NY: Cambridge University Press.

Baumrind, D. (1991) 'Effective Parenting during the Early Adolescent Transition.' In P.A. Cowan and E.M. Hetherington (eds) *Family Transitions.* Hillsdale, NJ: Lawrence Erlbaum.

Bell, R.Q. and Chapman, M. (1986) 'Child effects in studies using experimental or brief longitudinal approaches to socialization.' *Developmental Psychology 22,* 5, 595–603.

Borduin, C.M., Mann, B.J., Cone, L.T., Henggeler, S.W. *et al.* (1995) 'Multisystemic treatment of serious juvenile offenders: Long-term prevention of criminality and violence.' *Journal of Consulting and Clinical Psychology 63,* 4, 569–578.

Bronfenbrenner, U. (1979) *The Ecology of Human Development: Experiments by Nature and by Design.* Cambridge, MA: Harvard University Press.

Bronfenbrenner, U. (1986) 'Ecology of family as a context for human development perspectives.' *Development Psychology 22,* 6, 723–742.

Bronfenbrenner, U. (1989) 'Ecological Systems Theory.' In R. Vasta (ed.) *Six Theories of Child Development: Revised Formulations and Current Issues.* Greenwich, CT: JAI.

Bruyn, S.T. and Rayman, P. (1979) *Nonviolent Action and Social Change.* New York, NY: Irrington Publishers.

Bugental, D.B., Blue, J.B., Cortez, V., Fleck, K. *et al.* (1993) 'Social cognitions as organizers of autonomic and affective responses to social challenge.' *Journal of Personality and Social Psychology 64,* 1, 94–103.

Bugental, D.B. and Happaney, K. (2000) 'Parent-child interaction as a power contest.' *Journal of Applied Developmental Psychology 21,* 3, 267–282.

Bugental, D.B., Lyon, J.E., Kranz, J. and Cortez, V. (1997) Who's the boss? Accessibility of dominance ideation among individuals with low perceptions of interpersonal power.' *Journal of Personality and Social Psychology 72,* 6, 1297–1309.

Cairns, R.B., Santoyo, C.V. and Holly, K.A. (1994) 'Aggressive escalation: Toward a Developmental Analysis.' In M. Potegal and J.F. Knutson (eds) *The Dynamics of Aggression: Biological and Social Processes in Dyads and Groups.* Hillsdale, NJ: Lawrence Erlbaum.

Caspi, A., Elder, G.H. and Bem, D.J. (1987) 'Moving against the world: Life-course patterns of explosive children.' *Development Psychology 23,* 2, 308–313.

Cavell, T.A. (2001) 'Updating our approach to parental training: I. The case against targeting noncompliance.' *Clinical Psychology: Science and Practice 8,* 3, 299–318.

Chamberlain, P. and Patterson, G.R. (1995) 'Discipline and Child Compliance in Parenting.' In M.H. Bornstein (ed.) *Handbook of Parenting (Vol. 1).* Mahwah, NJ: Lawrence Erlbaum.

Charney, I.W. (ed.) (1978) *Strategies Against Violence: Design for Nonviolent Change.* Boulder, CO: Westview Press.

Cicchetti, D. and Lynch, M. (1993) 'Toward an ecological-transactional model of community violence and child maltreatment: Consequences for children's development.' *Psychiatry 56,* 1, 96–119.

Dagenais, D. (2008) *The (Un)Making of the Modern Family.* Translated by J. Brierley. Vancouver: University of British Colombia Press.

de Waal, F.B.M. (1993) 'Reconciliation among Primates: A Review of Empirical Evidence and Unresolved Issues.' In W.A. Mason and S.P. Mendoza (eds) *Primate Social Conflict.* New York, NY: State University of New York Press.

Dishion, T.J., French, D.C. and Patterson, G.R. (1995) 'The Development and Ecology of Antisocial Behaviour.' In D. Cicchetti and D.J. Cohen (eds) *Developmental Psychopathology, Vol. 2: Risk, Disorder and Adaptation.* New York, NY: John Wiley and Sons.

Dishion, T.J. and Patterson, G.R. (1992) 'Age effects in parent-training outcome.' *Behaviour Therapy 23,* 4, 719–729.

Eisenberg, N. and Murphy, B. (1995) 'Parenting and Children's Moral Development.' In M.H. Bornstein (ed.) *Handbook of Parenting (Vol. 1).* Mahwah, NJ: Lawrence Erlbaum.

Elkind, D. (1994) *Ties That Stress: The New Family Imbalance.* Cambridge, MA: Harvard University Press.

Farson, R. (1974) *Birthright: A Bill of Rights for Children.* New York, NY: Macmillan.

Fisher, R., Ury, W. and Paton, B. (1981) *Getting to Yes.* New York, NY: Random House.

Flowers, A.F., Schneider, H.G. and Ludtke, H.A. (1996) 'Social support and adjustment in mothers with young children.' *Journal of Divorce and Remarriage 25,* 69–83.

Forehand, R.L. and McMahon, R.J. (1981) *Helping the Noncompliant Child: A Clinician's Guide to Parent Training.* New York, NY: Guilford.

Hagerman, R. and Hagerman, P. (2002) *Fragile X Syndrome: Diagnosis, Treatment, and Research.* Baltimore, MD: Johns Hopkins Series in Contemporary Medicine and Public Health.

Jackson, D. (1965) 'The study of the family.' *Family Process 4,* 1, 1–20.

Kagan, J. (1997) 'Temperament and the reaction to unfamiliarity.' *Child Development 68,* 1, 139–143.

Kazdin, A.E. (1996) *Conduct Disorders in Childhood and Adolescence.* Thousand Oaks, CA: Sage.

Kazdin, A.E., Holland, L. and Crowley, M. (1997) 'Family experience of barriers to treatment and premature termination from child therapy.' *Journal of Consulting and Clinical Psychology 65*, 3, 453–463

Keltner, D. and Potegal, M. (1997) 'Appeasement and reconciliation: Introduction to an *Aggressive Behaviour* special issue.' *Aggressive Behavior 23*, 309–314.

Lewinsohn, P.M., Rohde, P. and Farrington, D.P. (2000) 'The OADP-CDS: A brief screener for adolescent conduct disorder.' *Journal of the American Academy of Child and Adolescent Psychiatry 39*, 77, 888–895.

Lynam, D., Moffitt, T. and Stouthamer-Loeber, M. (1993) 'Explaining the relation between IQ and delinquency: Class, race, test motivation, school failure, or self-control?' *Journal of Abnormal Psychology 102*, 2, 187–196.

Magnusson, D. (1988) 'Aggressiveness, Hyperactivity, and Automatic Activity/Reactivity in the Development of Social Maladjustment.' In D. Magnusson (ed.) *Paths Through Life: Individual Development from an Interactionary Perspective: A Longitudinal Study (Vol. 1).* Hillsdale, NJ: Lawrence Erlbaum.

Martin, R.P., Wisenbaker, J. and Huttunen, M. (1994) 'Review of Factor Analytic Studies of Temperament Measures based on the Chess-Thomas Model: Implications for the Big Five.' In C.F. Halverson, Jr., G.A. Kohnstamm and R.P. Martin (eds) *The Developing Structure of Temperament and Personality from Infancy to Adulthood.* Hillsdale, NJ: Lawrence Erlbaum.

Mccoby, E.E. and Martin, J.A. (1983) 'Socialization in the Context of the Family. Parent–Child Interaction.' In P.H. Mussen (Series Editor) and E.M. Hetherington (Volume Editor) *Handbook of Child Psychology: Socialization, Personality and Social Development (Fourth Edition, Vol. 4).* New York, NY: Wiley.

McCord, W., McCord, J. and Zola, I.K. (1959) *Origins of Crime.* New York, NY: Columbia University Press.

Miller, A. (1981) *Prisoners of Childhood.* New York, NY: Basic Books.

Miller, A. (1985) *Bilder einer kindheit.* Frankfurt am Main: Suhrkamp Verlag (In German.)

Minuchin, S. (1974) *Families and Family Therapy.* Cambridge, MA: Harvard University Press.

Mishler, E. and Waxler, N. (1966) 'Family interaction process and schizophrenia: A review of current theories.' *Archives of General Psychiatry 15*, 1, 64–74.

Moffitt, T.E. (1990) 'The Neuropsychology of Delinquency: A Critical Review of Theory and Research.' In N. Morris and M. Torny (eds) *Crime and Justice (Vol. 12).* Chicago, IL: University of Chicago Press.

Moffitt, T.E. (1993a) 'Adolescence-limited and life-course-persistent anti-social behavior: A developmental taxonomy.' *Psychological Review 100*, 4, 674–701.

Moffitt, T.E. (1993b) 'The neuropsychology of conduct disorder.' *Development and Psychopathology 5*, 135–151.

Neill, A.S. (1964) *Summerhill: A Radical Approach to Child Rearing.* New York, NY: Hart.

Olweus, D. (1980) 'Familial and temperamental determinants of aggressive behaviour in adolescent boys: A causal analysis.' *Developmental Psychology 16*, 6, 644–660.

Olweus, D. (1987) 'Testosterone Adrenaline: Aggressive Antisocial Behavior in Normal Adolescent Males.' In S.A. Mednick, T.E. Moffitt and S.A. Stack (eds) *The Causes of Crime: New Biological Approaches.* New York, NY: Cambridge University Press.

Omer, H. (2000) *Parental Presence.* Tel-Aviv: Modan Publishing House Ltd. (In Hebrew.)

Omer, H. (2001) 'Helping parents deal with children's acute disciplinary problems without escalation: The principle of non-violent resistance.' *Family Process 40*, 1, 53–66.

Omer, H., Weinblatt, U. and Avraham-Krehwinkel, C. (2002) 'Practising Non-violent Resistance in the Family Context.' In H. Omer (ed.) *The Struggle Against Children's Violence.* Tel-Aviv: Modan Publishing House Ltd. (In Hebrew.)

Parsons, T. (1965) 'The Normal American Family.' In S.M. Ferber, P. Mustacchi and R.H.L. Wilson (eds) *Man and Civilization: The Family's Search for Survival.* New York, NY: McGraw-Hill.

Patterson, G.R. (1976) *Living with Children: New Methods for Parents and Teachers.* Champaign, IL: Research Press.

Patterson, G.R. (1982) *Coercive Family Process.* Eugene, OR: Castalia.

Patterson, G.R. (1983) 'Stress: A Change Agent for Family Process.' In N. Garmezy and M. Rutter (eds) *Stress, Coping, and Development in Children.* New York, NY: McGraw-Hill.

Patterson, G.R. and Dishion, T.J. (1988) 'Multilevel Modes of Family Process: Traits, Interactions and Relationships.' In R. Hinde and J. Stevenson-Hinde (eds) *Relationships and Families: Mutual Influences.* Oxford, England: Clarendon Press.

Patterson, G.R., Dishion, T.J. and Bank, L. (1984) 'Family interaction: A process model of deviancy training.' *Aggressive Behavior 10,* 4, 253–267.

Patterson, G.R., Dishion, T.J. and Chamberlain, P. (1993) 'Outcomes and Methodological Issues Relating to Treatment of Antisocial Children.' In T.R. Giles (ed.) *Effective Psychotherapy: A Handbook of Comparative Research.* New York, NY: Plenum.

Patterson, G.R., Reid, J.B. and Dishion, T.J. (1992) *Antisocial Boys: A Social Interactional Approach.* Eugene, OR: Castalia.

Pepler, D. and Rubin, K. (eds) (1991) *The Development and Treatment of Childhood Aggression.* Hillsdale, NJ: Lawrence Erlbaum.

Quay, H.C. (1987) 'Patterns of Delinquent Behavior.' In H.C. Quay (ed.) *Handbook of Juvenile Delinquency.* New York, NY: Wiley.

Rende, R.D. (1993) 'Longitudinal relations between temperament traits and behavioral syndromes in middle childhood.' *Journal of the American Academy of Child and Adolescent Psychiatry 32,* 2, 287–290.

Rende, R.D. and Plomin, R. (1992) 'Diathesis-stress models of psychopathology: A quantitative perspective.' *Applied and Preventative Psychology 1,* 4, 177–182.

Rothbart, M.K. and Bates, J.E. (1998) 'Temperament.' In W. Damon (Series Editor) and N. Eisenberg (Volume Editor) *Handbook of Child Psychology: Vol. 3. Social, Emotional, and Personality Development (Fifth Edition).* New York, NY: Wiley.

Sameroff, A. and Chandler, M. (1975) 'Reproductive Risk and the Continuum of Caretaking Casualty.' In F. Horowitz, M. Hetherington, S. Scarr-Salapatek and G. Siegel (eds) *Review of Child Development Research (Vol. 4).* Chicago, IL: University of Chicago Press.

Sharp, G. (1960) *Gandhi Wields the Weapon of Moral Power: Three Case Histories.* Ahmedabad: Navajivan Publishing House.

Sharp, G. (1973) *The Politics of Nonviolent Action.* Boston, MA: Extending Horizons Books.

Spiker, D., Kraemer, H.C., Constantine, N.A. and Bryant, D. (1992) 'Reliability and validity of behavior problem checklists as measures of stable traits in low birth weight premature preschoolers.' *Child Development 63,* 6, 1481–1496.

Spock, B. and Parker, S. (1998) *Baby and Child Care. A Handbook for Parents of the Developing Child from Birth through Adolescence (Revised and Updated Seventh Edition).* New York, NY: Penguin Putnam.

Thomas, A. and Chess, S. (1977) *Temperament and Development.* New York, NY: Brunner/Mazel.

Tremblay, R.E., McCord, J., Boileau, H., Charlebois, P. *et al.* (1991) 'Can disruptive boys be helped to become competent?' *Psychiatry 54,* 148–161.

Wiggins, J., Dill, F. and Schwartz, R. (1965) 'On 'status liability'.' *Sociometry 28,* 2, 197–209.

Index

Adler, Alfred 83
aggression 15–16
    and attachment model
        18–19
    and Schmidt family 49–53
Aldridge, D. 11, 20, 21, 22,
    24, 25, 32, 42, 43
anti-social behaviour
    and aggression 15–16
    and attachment model
        18–19
    and Non-Violent Resistance
        approach 33–4
    origins of 15
    and temperament 16–17
attachment model 17–19
authoritarian parenting styles
    13
Avraham-Krehwinkel, C. 10,
    12, 44, 142

Bandura, A. 15, 38
Bates, J.E. 10, 16, 29
Baumrind, D. 13
Bell, R.Q. 17
Bem, D.J. 17
Borduin, C.M. 10
Bronfenbrenner, U. 11
Bruyn, S.T. 10, 30, 34, 36
Bugental, D.B. 10

Cairns, R.B. 10, 40
case studies
    Braun family 80–108
    Halpern family 109–27
    Hernandez family 62–79
    Schmidt family 48–61
    Werner family 128–41
Caspi, A. 17
Cavell, T.A. 10, 38
Chamberlain, P. 9, 10, 13,
    15, 18
Chandler, M. 17
Chapman, M. 17
Charney, I.W. 36

Chess, S. 15
Cicchetti, D. 17
coercion theory 10, 46–7
conflict
    and Non-Violent Resistance
        approach 35–6, 144–7
Cortez, V. 10
Crowley, M. 9

Dagenais, D. 174
de Waal, F.B.M. 11
declaration of intent
    and Braun family 93–4,
        95–6
    and Halpern family 122–4
    and Hernandez family
        69–71, 72–3
    and Non-Violent Resistance
        approach 147–50
    and Schmidt family 55–6
    and Werner family 134–5
deviant behaviour
    and eco-systems approach
        20–3, 31–2
    understanding of 30–1
Dill, F. 22
Dishion, T.J. 9, 10, 17, 30
distress
    and Non-Violent Resistance
        approach 43, 45–6
    systemic management of
        23–8
Dodge, K.A. 29

eco-systems approach
    and deviant behaviour
        20–3, 31–2
    and Non-Violent Resistance
        approach 11, 44
    and parent–child
        relationships 20–3
Eisenberg, N. 13, 40
Elder, G.H. 17
Elkind, D. 14
escalation of demands 142–3

and Halpern family
    115–18
and Non-Violent Resistance
    approach 10–11, 34–5,
    44–5, 144, 181–2
and parent–child
    relationships 11
and Schmidt family 52–3

Farrington, D.P. 17
Farson, R. 14
Fisher, R. 40
Flowers, A.F. 28
Forehand, R.L. 29
Freeland, C.A.B. 16
French, D.C. 10

Gandhi, Mahatma 10, 35, 36
gender roles
    and Non-Violent Resistance
        approach 182–3
Guidebook for Parents 44, 53,
    54, 55, 66, 67, 87, 101,
    105, 178–80

Hagerman, P. 15
Hagerman, R. 15
Happaney, K. 10
Holland, L. 9
Holly, K.A. 10
Huttunen, M. 15

Jackson, D. 23

Kagan, J. 30
Kazdin, A.E. 9, 14, 15
Keltner, D. 11
King, Martin Luther 10,
    35, 36

Lewinsohn, P.M. 17
linking
    and Non-Violent Resistance
        approach 158–61
Lounsbury, M.L. 16
Ludtke, H.A. 28

Lynam, D. 15
Lynch, M. 17
Lyon, J.E. 10

Magnusson, D. 16
Martin, R.P. 15, 17
Mccoby, E.E. 17
McCord, J. 13
McCord, W. 13
McMahon, R.J. 29
Miller, A. 14
Minuchin, S. 11
Mishler, E. 21
Moffitt, T.E. 10, 15
Murphy, B. 13, 40

Neill, A.S. 14
Non-Violent Resistance
approach
and Braun family 81–108
and coercion theory 10,
46–7
conditions for 9–10
and conflict 35–6, 144–7
and confrontation 39–40
declaration of intent
147–50
and eco-systems approach
11, 44
and escalation of demands
10–11, 34–5, 44–5,
144, 181–2
and gender roles 182–3
and Halpern family
109–27
and Hernandez family
66–79
and intention of the subject
30
as intervention 10
linking 158–61
and parent–child
relationships 43–6, 144
and parental authority
37–41
political position 10, 35–6
practice of 43–6
principles of 10, 30, 33–4
and reconciliation 169–70
and responsibility 183–4
and Schmidt family 53–61
and sit-down strike 161–9
'sit-in' activity 150–5
and social networks 155–8
stages of 47

success of 9, 11–12
and Werner family 128–41

Olweus, D. 13, 16
Omer, H. 37, 142

parent–child relationships
and Braun family 80–8, 90
and eco-systems approach
20–3
and escalation of demands
11
fear of change in 177–8
and Hernandez family
62–4
and Non-Violent Resistance
approach 43–6, 144
and parenting styles 13,
14–15
and Schmidt family 49–53
and school 128–41
and social networks 28–9
and systemic management
of distress 23–8
and Werner family 128–41
parental authority
and confrontation 39–40
and Non-Violent Resistance
approach 37–41
and secrecy 40–1
parental coaching 29
parenting styles
authoritarian approach 13
effect on child behaviour
13, 14–15
and parental coaching 29
pendulum approach 14–15
permissive approach 13, 14
Parker, S. 14
Parsons, T. 14
Paton, B. 40
Patterson, G.R. 9, 10, 11, 13,
14, 15, 17, 18, 38, 40
pendulum parenting styles
14–15
Pepler, D. 15
permissive parenting styles
13, 14
Pettit, G.S. 29
Plomin, R. 15
Potegal, M. 11
psychotherapy 174–5

Rayman, P. 10, 30, 34, 36
reconciliation

and Halpern family 125–6
and Non-Violent Resistance
approach 169–70
Reid, J.B. 10
Rende, R.D. 15
Rohde, P. 17
Rothbart, M.K. 10
Rubin, K. 15

Sameroff, A. 17
Santoyo, C.V. 10
Schneider, H.G. 28
school
and parent–child
relationships 128–41
Schwartz, R. 22
Sharp, G. 10, 37
sit-down strike
and Non-Violent Resistance
approach 161–9
'sit-in' activity 150–5
and Werner family 134
social interaction 17
social networks 28–9
and Braun family 103–5
and Halpern family 123–4
and Non-Violent Resistance
approach 155–8
Spiker, D. 30
Spock, B. 14
Stouthamer-Loeber, M. 15
systemic management of
distress
and parent–child
relationships 23–8

temperament 16–17
Thomas, A. 15
Tremblay, R.E. 15

Ury, W. 40

Waxler, N. 21
Weinblatt, U. 142
Wiggins, J. 22
Wisenbaker, J. 15

Zola, I.K. 13